JOURNEYS NEAR AND FAR 2
Reading and Responding Critically

Linda Best
Kean University

Jessie M. Reppy
Kean University

Houghton Mifflin Company
Boston ◆ New York

Director, World Languages: Marketing and ESL Publishing   Susan Maguire
Senior Associate Editor   Kathy Sands Boehmer
Editorial Assistant   Manuel Muñoz
Senior Project Editor   Kathryn Dinovo
Senior Cover Design Coordinator   Deborah Azerrad Savona
Senior Manufacturing Coordinator   Marie Barnes
Marketing Manager   Jay Hu
Marketing Associate   Claudia Martínez

Cover design   Rebecca Fagan
Cover image   Tana Powell

Photo credits   **p. 1:** © Tom & Dee Ann McCarthy/The Stock Market. **p. 7:** © Andy Powell.
p. 17: © STONE/Lawrence Migdale. **p. 28:** © PhotoDisc, Inc. **p. 37 (top):** © PhotoDisc, Inc.
p. 37 (right): Photo: www.comstock.com. **p. 37 (bottom):** © CORBIS. **p. 37 (left):** © Anthony Edgeworth/
The Stock Market. **p. 42:** © STONE/Jim Corwin. **p. 51:** Illustration by Judy Love. **p. 63:** © Balaguer/
CORBIS Sygma. **p. 77:** Fred R. Conrad/The New York Times Pictures. **p. 85:** Illustration by Judy Love.
p. 89: © STONE/Terry Vine. **p. 95:** © Illustration by Judy Love. **p. 98:** Illustration by Judy Love.
p. 108: Illustration by Judy Love. **p. 118:** © AP/Wide World Photos. **p. 119:** © AP/Wide World Photos.
p. 129: © AP/Wide World Photos. **p. 133:** © AP/Wide World Photos. **p. 142:** © CORBIS. **p. 143:** © AP/Wide
World Photos. **p. 154:** Illustration by Judy Love. **p. 156:** Illustration by Judy Love. **p. 160:** © Hulton
Getty/Liaison. **p. 167:** © Phototake/Michael Freeman. **p. 171:** Illustration by Judy Love. **p. 181:** The Country
Life Picture Library. **p. 189:** Illustration by Judy Love. **p. 201:** Laurence Best.

http://college.hmco.com

Printed in the U.S.A.

Library of Congress Catalog Card Number   00-104718

ISBN   0-395-97693-6

3456789-QF-05 04 03 02 01

As part of Houghton Mifflin's ongoing
commitment to the environment, this text
has been printed on recycled paper.

In loving memory of my parents, Anthony and Lena Buzzeo,
who inspired me from the start; for Barbara and Michael Best,
for accepting and taking pride in my work; and especially for
Larry Best—a great listener and a creative, critical thinker—
without whom my work would lack focus and luster.

Linda Best

To John P. Keker, whose interest, assistance, and
encouragement enabled me to complete our two-book project.

Jessie M. Reppy

CONTENTS

INTRODUCTION

Journeys Near and Far: Reading and Responding Critically is a two-book interactive reading series with a writing component. Book 1 is directed to students at the intermediate level, and Book 2 to students at the high-intermediate level. The series is designed for students learning English in academic programs at the postsecondary level. A strong theoretical base and a cognitive orientation support the content, varied activities, and attention to critical thinking in the series.

Thought-provoking reading selections, diverse in their perspectives, are arranged thematically, appealing to students' sense of the familiar at first and then guiding them to explore the distant and less familiar. Book 2 opens with Chapter 1, "The People, Places, and Experiences That Shape Identity;" selections include a young man's story of his mixed heritage, a woman's memories of her native country, and a journalist's experiences with the customs of another country. Chapter 2, "Pathways and Passages: Exploring Our Human Stories," examines different stages of life and the decisions individuals must make through Robert Frost's "The Road Not Taken," a story about an arranged marriage, a narrative by a female revolutionary in Guatemala, and an account of six successful college-bound students who overcame adversity to reach their goals. "The Heroes in Our Lives," Chapter 3, explores who can be a hero with stories about local heroes, acts of generosity, and the contributions of Princess Diana. Chapter 4 examines human behavior in difficult circumstances. Entitled "Coping with Tragedy and Destruction," the chapter illustrates scenes of destruction in different parts of the world during different times—from Hurricane Mitch to the explosion of the shuttle *Challenger* to a concentration camp in Argentina. The final chapter, "Exploring Strange Events," focuses on events that are not only distant and abstract but beyond reasonable explanation—visionary encounters, ghosts, ESP, and the Bermuda Triangle.

These chapters are linked by their common format, yet they remain independent of one another. Multiple sequences for presenting them are possible; the order of presentation can vary to account for factors affecting the classroom experience: guests on campus, an orientation or campus event theme, students' interests, or material covered in a concurrent course, for example. All supporting sections emphasize the students' active role in the learning process. Activities in these sections engage students in the thoughtful reading and reflection that stimulate interest, promote inquiry, facilitate comprehension, aid developing reading strategies and vocabulary, generate critical oral and written response, and inspire confidence. The chapters in the book contain some or all of the following activities:

- **Opening Thought**
  A quotation or concept and follow-up questions that guide students to discover the chapter's purpose

- **Discover What You Know, Think, Feel**
  A series of questions that guide students to explore their knowledge about a selection's topic

- **Previewing**
  An introduction to the selection, which consists of a series of questions in Chapters 1 and 2, and an independent activity in the remaining chapters

- **Quick Comprehension Check**
  A summary of the selection's content, which is a fill-in-the-blank activity in the first two chapters and an activity for developing summarizing skills in the remaining chapters

- **Questions for Thought and Discussion**
  A series of questions probing the selection's meaning, purpose, and relevance

- **Another Look at the Selection**
  An activity for examining closely a specific idea in a passage from the selection

- **Looking Beyond the Selection**
  A new section for Chapters 4 and 5 that includes supplemental reading and research activities

- **Vocabulary Building**
  Exercises or activities for using or adding to vocabulary in the selection

- **In Your Words**
  Different activities for retelling parts of the selections or formulating opinions about them

- **Summing Up**
  A series of questions summarizing the class's work with and discussion about a selection's topics

- **Reflecting and Synthesizing**
  A section that guides students to explore how material from the chapter relates to their lives and experiences

The activities in the different sections are varied. They include prereading questions, comprehension activities, discussion questions, match columns, self-monitoring, Internet research, summarizing activities, oral activities, double-entry journals, logs, writing activities, vocabulary study in context, work with synonyms and antonyms, creating tables and charts, writing dialogue, role play, and debate. Activities can be completed in a number of ways and are suitable for group, pair, class, or independent work.

Every selection in each chapter is an authentic piece, written at a certain moment in time to tell a story or express a feeling. Guided by Freire's pedagogy and Vygotsky's theories, we have not reduced the vocabulary in any of these selections. We have retained their rich sense, provided glossaries as well as vocabulary exercises for each selection, and stressed the importance of reading to understand the sense of a selection.

To the Student

The many students we have worked with inspired us to write *Journeys Near and Far: Reading and Responding Critically*. Our students wanted fresh and challenging material. They helped us understand what you might be interested in reading as you work to develop your English language skills. We hope you enjoy the selections, are inspired to respond to them, expand your vocabulary by reading and responding, and feel confident about what you have to say.

Linda Best and Jessie M. Reppy

ACKNOWLEDGMENTS

We extend our special thanks to the faculty, staff, and students of the English as a Second Language Program at Kean University, who are all part of the academic context that supported the design and development of the two-book series *Journeys Near and Far: Reading and Responding Critically.* We are especially grateful to the English as a Second Language students at Kean University, who represent 55 countries. Their insights and input guided the preparation of our materials and generated our motivation as well.

In addition, we thank Susan Maguire, Director of English as a Second Language Programs, for supporting our vision for the project; Kathy Sands-Boehmer, Senior Associate Editor, for her expertise, guidance, and input; and Manuel Muñoz, Editorial Assistant, for help with the process of preparing and submitting our manuscript. Moreover, we gratefully acknowledge the thoughtful critiques and suggestions from the following reviewers: Victoria Badalamenti, LaGuardia Community College; John Bagnole, OPIE/Ohio University; Ron Clark, CELOP/Boston University; Janet Eveler, El Paso Community College; Frank Hermann, Houston Community College; Kathy Judd, Truman College; and Beth Pullman, DeKalb Technical Institute.

We also thank Dr. Betsy Rodriguez-Bachiller of Kean University for her professional and technical assistance as well as Barbara and Michael Best for their thought-provoking ideas and technical support.

1

THE PEOPLE, PLACES, AND EXPERIENCES THAT SHAPE IDENTITY

OPENING THOUGHT

> *. . . A man's self is the sum total of all he can call his . . .*

William James *The Principles of Psychology* (1890)

Think about the chapter's title, quotation, and opening photograph. Answer the following questions:

1. Examine the photograph and select one person from the group. Tell what you know or might guess about this person based on his or her image in the photograph.

   _____

   _____

   _____

   _____

2. Read the quotation carefully and restate it in your own words.

   _____

   _____

   _____

   _____

3. Tell what you know about the chapter's topic. Use personal experiences, what you know about other people, and information from your studies and reading.

   _____

   _____

   _____

   _____

4. Tell what you expect to read about in this chapter.

_____

_____

_____

_____

5. Give basic information about your identity, such as your name, gender, age, ethnic background, native country, current residence, interests, and hobbies.

_____

_____

_____

_____

Share your thoughts with your partner, group, or class.

The selections in this chapter focus on identity. Read about how the authors recognize themselves as individuals and then analyze the circumstances that shaped their individuality. Consider the identity of particular groups of people. Your work with the selections involves strategies for reading effectively—for understanding, recalling, restating, and analyzing what you read.

> **COURSE LOG:** Your work also includes a **course log.** In a notebook, write your thoughts about the selections, your questions about unfamiliar words, and your word lists. Your course log is **both** a journal and a vocabulary log. Enter information in it for a number of reasons—because you have ideas you want to record, because you are following the directions of a particular exercise, or because you are guided to do so by your instructor. Include illustrations, such as your own drawings or photographs from newspapers and magazines. Remember to date all your entries so that you can locate information easily, when necessary, and so that you can get a sense of your reading skills and strategies over a period of time.

Selection 1

DISCOVER WHAT YOU KNOW

1. What is an interracial marriage?

2. How do people in the United States regard individuals of diverse racial and ethnic backgrounds?

3. What is the relationship between race and identity?

PREVIEWING

People often preview something before reading it to get a general idea of what it is about. If you browse in a bookstore or library, for example, you can preview books or magazines to see if they appeal to or interest you. Every day, millions of people preview newspapers to identify articles they want or need to read.

When you preview reading material, you look it over quickly. You may focus on particular sections, such as the beginning or the end, accompanying photographs, or changes in print style or size. This brief process enables you, the reader, to see a selection's organization, its layout, and key words. Knowing about these will help you comprehend material when reading it closely. The following questions will help you focus your preview of this first selection:

1. **a.** What is the title?

   _____

   b. What information does this title give you?

   _____

   c. What information do you need?

   _____

2. **a.** Who is the author?

   _____

   b. What do you know about this author?

   _____

3. a. Where did this selection appear?

_____

    b. What do you know about this source?

_____

4. a. Are there any illustrations? _____ What do you see in the
illustration?

_____

    b. How does the illustration relate to the selection's title?

_____

5. a. Are there any words in bold print? _____ Do you understand these
words? _____ If not, list the words you do not understand.

_____

_____

    b. What do you think the words you listed might mean?

_____

6. a. Quickly read the first and last paragraphs of the article. What is the first
paragraph about?

_____

_____

    b. What is the last paragraph about?

_____

7. Now scan the remaining paragraphs. From this quick review, write what you
think about the selection. For example, do you think the selection will be
interesting? Will you have difficulty reading it? Do you have any sense of the
characters' feelings or attitudes?

_____

_____

8. What do you know about the characters in the story?

_____

_____

_____

9. What questions do you have now that you have previewed the selection?

_____

_____

_____

MY FATHER'S BLACK PRIDE

    I am black, my mother is black. My father is white. This wouldn't necessarily be important, but we live in a country where conflict runs deep between blacks and whites. We live in a country where white male slaveholders casually **disavowed** the black children they had **sired.** We live in a country where the worst of human traits—laziness, violence, and irrationality—are seen as defining characteristics of those of African descent. This makes my being a mixed-race person whose ethnic identity is black somewhat complicated. There is a **dissonance** between who I say I am—a proud black man trying to do something positive with his life—and who society says I am. Yet I feel strong, and I **embrace** my black heritage. I've often reflected on how I learned to keep my positive self-image. The answer is, my white father.

    With my olive-colored skin, hazel eyes and curly hair, I've been taken for Hispanic or Middle Eastern. In fact, in addition to being black, I am Jewish. And my father taught me to be proud of that heritage as well. When bullies at school demanded, "Are you black or white?" there was no confusion. When I ran home and asked my father, he said, "Tell them you are African-American." That was in the early 1970's and it was a term I wouldn't hear until the Afrocentric movement of the 1990's made it fashionable again.

    It wasn't that my father wanted me to deny my Jewish roots, it's just that he knew we live in a society where my African heritage would define me socially. He didn't want me to seem ashamed of my black roots. My father knew that love and hopes for an ideal world in the distant future

would be no **panacea** for the **bigotry** and small-mindedness I would
encounter in my lifetime. He didn't want me, my brother or my sister to be
unprepared for racism.

And so, my father, a writer and **avid** reader, lined my shelves with books
about American culture, African culture and Jewish culture. He encouraged
me to think, to come up with my own ideas. A simple question posed to
him was sure to be followed by his search for a book on the subject, with
articles and additional materials to follow. In this way he gave me not only
his opinion, but also the keys to how he arrived at that opinion. Knowing
that I had those keys, too, he thought that I could evaluate his opinion and
come up with my own. He encouraged me to determine what being black
meant to me.

In the **predominantly** white suburb near Princeton, N.J., where I grew
up, my father knew that I needed to know black men. So when I started
playing drums at age 14, my father took me to jazz clubs. He encouraged me
to talk to the musicians and get their autographs. This introduction led to my
decision to become a professional musician, and also filled my home with a
black male presence.

Jazz was more than a
genre of music; it
instructed me in the cool
posture of black men—
Max Roach's shades,
Miles Davis's **scowl** and
his always stylish
threads. It also instructed
me in a kind of heroism.
These men were geniuses
who created America's
only enduring art form
despite its best efforts to
stifle and ignore them.

My father also hired
James, a black 16-year-
old, who became my
favorite baby sitter. My
father gave me book
knowledge and taught
me to have an open
mind; James showed me
how to deal with people on

An abstract image of the
author's mixed heritage

65 a practical level. My father was gentle, but James taught me that as a black man, you have to be ungentle sometimes. You have to speak up for yourself. James never let me walk away from a confrontation without speaking my mind.

70 During the summers, my parents sent me to my mother's family in Virginia. My cousins—especially Jeffrey, who is seven years older than I—helped me become a mature black man. Jeffrey taught me to treat women with respect, through his example as well as through his words. These are lessons my father had taught me also, but he hoped that my summer visits down South would reinforce those values by being transmitted by black men **75** of my generation.

In college, I counseled children from mixed backgrounds. I could see the emptiness in some of the kids either who didn't have a black parent around—usually the father—or whose parents weren't in agreement about how much emphasis should be put on black culture. Often these children **80** would grow up in a **predominantly** white environment with a negative view of their black fathers or of black culture in general. I realized how fortunate I was to have both parents and to have a father who encouraged me to develop as a black person while never making me feel that I was any less his son because of my blackness.

85 In many ways what my father taught me about manhood was not related to color. He taught me that, ultimately, I determined through my behavior what a black man is. My father taught me to be a gentle man, to use my mind and not my fists. He taught me the value of education and encouraged me to ask questions. My father exposed me to black men who lived up to **90** these universal ideals of manhood, and thereby emphasized that blacks shared in that tradition. All these things have made me the man, the black man, I am today.

My father and I are now the closest we have ever been. Of course, there are race-related topics, things I feel, that he will never be able to understand. **95** I know that there are probably people who meet my father and see just another white man. But I know that there are things he has learned from me and my brother that have given him an insight into black masculinity that most white men will never experience. In this way, we have taught each other. Our relationship **epitomizes** a reality that is so rarely seen—a black **100** man and a white man who are not adversaries. Who are more than father and son. They are men who love each other very deeply.

Marcus Bleecker
Copyright © 1995 by the New York Times, Co. Reprinted by permission.

GLOSSARY

avid (adj.) marked by keen interest and enthusiasm

bigotry (n.) intolerance; prejudice

disavow (v.) to deny knowledge of, responsibility for, or association with

dissonance (n.) lack of agreement, consistency, harmony; conflict

embrace (v.) to take up willingly or eagerly

epitomize (v.) to be a typical example of

genre (n.) a type or class

panacea (n.) a remedy for all diseases, evils, or difficulties; a cure-all

predominantly (adv.) mainly; primarily

scowl (n.) a look of anger or frowning disapproval

sire (v.) to father; to beget

QUICK COMPREHENSION CHECK ✅

The following paragraph offers a brief summary of the selection's content. Read it carefully and complete the sentences, using words and phrases from the answer bank below.

- James, the babysitter, and cousin Jeffrey
- his father
- his mother is black and his father is white
- color
- to be proud of his heritage, to come up with his own ideas, and to value education
- people view individuals of African descent as lazy, violent, and irrational
- positive
- the value of education and the importance of asking questions

The author identifies himself as a mixed-race person because **(1)** _____
_____. He explains that his heritage
could be a source of conflict in the United States, where **(2)** _____
_____. Overall, though,
the author has a **(3)** _____ self-image, which he learned
from **(4)** _____. Some of the things the
author learned from this individual are **(5)** _____
_____. Other people have influenced the
author as well. These people are **(6)** _____
_____. The author asserts that what he learned about
manhood is not about **(7)** _____.
Instead it involves certain ideals and goals, such as **(8)** _____
_____.

QUESTIONS FOR THOUGHT AND DISCUSSION

1. Did the material in the selection match what you expected to read when you previewed it? Explain your response.

2. What is Bleecker's ethnic background?

    Why does he regard it as a potential problem in American society?

3. What stereotype does Bleecker introduce in the first paragraph?

    How is this stereotype connected to his personal experience?

    Do you have any experience with the stereotype he describes?

4. Explore the reasons why Bleecker's father worked so hard to have his son understand his African heritage.

    What values and attitudes did Marcus learn from his father?

5. How did the author try to help people whose experiences with heritage and identity were similar to his?

6. What are possible sources of conflict between the author and his father? Why?

7. Little is said about Bleecker's mother.

   What do you know about her?

   What can you guess about her?

   Why is the selection more about father and son than mother, father, and son or mother and son?

8. What adjectives would you use to describe Marcus Bleecker?

9. What did you learn about the shaping of identity from this particular selection?

10. What question would you want to ask Marcus about his life, his father, his identity, or another topic?

ANOTHER LOOK AT THE SELECTION

Coordinating Conjunctions

So far, your work with this selection has focused on its content—the information the author shared and the message he wanted to convey. Now let's examine the way the author writes. The material is presented in strong, readable sentences. Analyzing some of these sentences to examine principles of language will be useful as you develop your English language skills. The author combines clauses using appropriate connecting words and correct punctuation in the following sentences.

A. Read the following sentences carefully.

   1. I feel strong, and I embrace my black heritage.

   2. My father was gentle, but James taught me . . . you have to be ungentle sometimes.

   3. These are lessons my father had taught me also, but he hoped . . . my summer visits down South would reinforce those values. . . .

B. Circle the connecting words in the preceding examples.

COORDINATING CONJUNCTIONS: The connecting words the author uses are **coordinating conjunctions.** Coordinating conjunctions connect two complete thoughts to improve the flow of writing and to strengthen the meaningful relationship between the thoughts.

These words can serve as coordinating conjunctions: *and, but, so, for, yet, or.*

TIP: A comma precedes any conjunction that connects two complete thoughts.

Example: I would like to travel to my country for the holidays, yet I do not have the time or money to do so.

C. Write two sentences of your own about Marcus Bleecker's story, using coordinating conjunctions to link thoughts. Circle your connecting words.

1. _____

   _____

2. _____

   _____

VOCABULARY BUILDING

Antonyms

What attitude does the author convey about himself and the people close to him? Overall, do you classify this attitude as positive or negative? Circle one response.

Positive   Negative

The words *positive* and *negative* are opposites. This exercise will give you practice with words and their opposites, or **antonyms.** An example is done for you in the chart. The word *embrace*, which the author uses to tell that he gladly accepts his African-American heritage, is paired with the word *reject*.

VOCABULARY STRATEGY: A word and its antonym should be the same part of speech. You should be able to substitute one for the other if you want to reverse the meaning of a sentence. Be sure that the antonyms you enter in the chart that follows are the same part of speech as the word with which you pair them.

A. Using your dictionary and working with a partner, write an antonym for each word in the chart.

POSITIVE	NEGATIVE
1. embrace (v.)	*reject* (v.)
2. respect (n.)	
3. proud (adj.)	
4. ideal (adj.)	
5. encourage (v.)	
6. open-minded (adj.)	
7.	conflict (n.)
8.	dissonance (n.)
9.	ashamed (adj.)
10.	stifle (v.)
11.	emptiness (n.)
12.	adversary (n.)

B. Get additional practice with antonyms. Create a section for new words in your course log. Identify this section with today's date. Divide the section into two columns. Label one column *new words* and the other column *antonyms*. For one week, enter new words you learn in this course and others into your course log. Then find an antonym for each. After one week, review your work and answer these questions:

- What new words and antonyms are you likely to use regularly?

- Will your word list and antonyms help with your course work in any way?

- Were there any words for which you could not find an appropriate antonym?

IN YOUR WORDS

Connecting Concepts

In the selection, the author establishes a connection between the concepts *heritage* and *identity*. On your own, with a partner, or in a small group, take a few moments to explore and respond to his ideas. Approach this exploration methodically by doing the following:

1. Explain what the word *heritage* means.

   _____

   _____

   _____

2. Explain how a person's *heritage* plays a role in *identity*.

   _____

   _____

   _____

3. Tell whether you agree with the author that *heritage* and *identity* are connected.

   _____

   _____

   _____

4. Describe a personal experience or incident that illustrates the connection between *heritage* and *identity*. Be specific about the information you share and include details that support the point you want to make.

   _____

   _____

   _____

SUMMING UP

Share your thoughts about the selection in a group or with the class. What do others think?

1. Did your classmates think that the selection's title matched its content?

2. What connection did your classmates see between the words *heritage* and *identity*?

   Did everyone agree on the connection between these two concepts? If so, summarize what the group said. If not, summarize the disagreement.

3. What is the group's definition of the word *identity*? What information about a person tells about his or her *identity*?

Selection 2

DISCOVER WHAT YOU KNOW

1. What are your fondest memories or thoughts about people and places in your country?

2. What customs from your country do you continue to practice today?

3. How have the people, places, and customs of your country played a part in the shaping of your identity?

PREVIEWING

To preview the selection, answer the following questions:

1. **a.** What is the title? _____

   _____

   b. What information do you get from this title?

   _____

   _____

    c. What is the possible connection between the selection's title and the chapter's title, "The People, Places, and Experiences That Shape Identity"?

_____

2. a. Are there any words in bold print? _____

    b. Do you understand these words? _____

    c. If not, which words are they? _____

_____

    d. How will you find the meanings for these words? _____

_____

3. a. Are there any photographs? _____ What do you see in the photograph?

_____

    b. How does the photograph relate to the selection's title? _____

_____

4. a. Quickly read the first and last paragraphs of the selection. What is the first paragraph about?

_____

    b. What is the last paragraph about? _____

_____

5. a. What do you see in the photograph for this selection? _____

_____

    b. What is the possible connection between the photograph and the selection?

_____

6. What do you know about the people in the story? _____

_____

7. What questions do you have about the selection? _____

_____

_____

KITCHENS from *Getting Home Alive*

I went into the kitchen just now to stir the black beans and rice, the shiny black beans floating over the smooth brown grains of rice and the zucchini turning black, too, in the ink of the beans. Mine is a California kitchen, full of fresh vegetables and whole grains, bottled spring water and yogurt in
5 plastic pints, but when I lift the lid from that big black pot, my kitchen fills with the hands of women who came before me, washing rice, washing beans, picking through them so deftly, so swiftly, that I could never see what the defects were in the beans they threw quickly over one shoulder out the window. Some instinct of the fingertips after years of sorting to feel the
10 rottenness of the bean with a worm in it or a chewed-out side. Standing here, I see the smooth red and brown and white and speckled beans sliding through their fingers into bowls of water, the gentle clicking rush of them being poured into the pot, hear the hiss of escaping steam, smell the bean scum floating on the surface under the lid. I see grains of rice settling in a
15 basin on the counter, turning the water milky with rice polish and the **talc** they use to make the grains so smooth; fingers dipping, swimming through the murky white water, feeling for the grain with the blackened tip, the brown stain.

From the corner of my eye, I see the knife blade flashing, reducing
20 mounds of onions, garlic, cilantro, and green peppers into sofrito to be fried up and stored, and best of all is the pound and circular grind of the pilón: *pound, pound, thump, grind, pound, pound, thump, grind. Pound, pound* (the

Three generations of a family working together

garlic and oregano mashed together), *THUMP!* (the mortar lifted and slammed down to loosen the crushed herbs and spices from the wooden bowl), *grind* (the slow rotation of the **pestle** smashing the **oozing** mash around and around, blending the juices, the green stain of cilantro and oregano, the sticky yellowing garlic, the grit of black pepper). . . .

It's a magic, a power, a **ritual** of love and work that rises up in my kitchen, thousands of miles from those women in cotton dresses who twenty years ago taught the rules of its observance to me, the **apprentice,** the **novice,** the girl-child: "Don't go without wrapping your head, child, you've been roasting coffee, y te va' a pa'mar!" "This much coffee in the colador, girl, or you'll be serving brown water." "Dip the basin in the river, so, to leave the mud behind." "Always peel the green bananas under cold water, mijita, or you'll cut your fingers and get mancha on yourself and the stain never comes out: that black sap stain of guineo verde and plátano, the stain that marks you forever."

So I peel my bananas under running water from the faucet, but the stain won't come out, and the subtle earthy green smell of that sap follows me, down from the mountains, into the cities, to places where banana groves are like a green dream, unimaginable by daylight: Chicago, New Hampshire, Oakland. So I travel miles on the bus to the immigrant markets of other people, coming home laden with bundles, and even, now and then, on the plastic frilled tables of the supermarket, I find a small curved green bunch to rush home, quick, before it ripens, to peel and boil, bathing in the scent of its cooking, bringing the river to flow through my own kitchen now, the river of my place on earth, the green and musty river of my grandmothers, dripping, trickling, tumbling down from the mountain kitchens of my people.

Excerpt from "Kitchens" in *Getting Home Alive* by Aurora Levins Morales and Rosario Morales. Copyright © 1986 Aurora Levins Morales and Rosario Morales. Reprinted by permission of Firebrand Books, Ithaca, New York.

GLOSSARY

apprentice (n.) a beginner; a learner

novice (n.) a person new to a field or activity; beginner

oozing (adj.) flowing or leaking out slowly, as through small openings

pestle (n.) a club-shaped tool for grinding or mashing substances in a bowl

ritual (n.) a ceremonial act or a series of such acts

talc (n.) a fine-grained white, greenish, or gray mineral having a soft soapy feel and used in talcum and face powder and as a filler in paper and plastics

QUICK COMPREHENSION CHECK ✓

The following paragraph offers a brief summary of the selection's content. Read it carefully and complete the sentences, using words and phrases from the answer bank.

- past
- rice and beans
- thoughts about the hands of the women who came before her, washing beans in their kitchens
- kitchen
- stories and experiences from 20 years before when she was a little girl

The woman in the story is in her California **(1)** _____

cooking **(2)** _____. As she lifts the lid of her big

black pot, her kitchen fills with **(3)** _____

_____

Her thoughts shift from the present to the **(4)** _____.

She remembers another place and other people. The memories she describes

include **(5)** _____

_____.

QUESTIONS FOR THOUGHT AND DISCUSSION

1. Picture the narrator in her California kitchen and tell what you see.
2. What adjectives would you use to describe her? Why?
3. Summarize some of the narrator's childhood memories and explain what role they played in the shaping of her identity.
4. Describe the grandmothers' kitchens, as you imagine them to be.

   Compare and contrast the grandmothers' kitchens to what you think you see in the narrator's California kitchen.
5. What type of relationship does the narrator have with her family? How do you know this?

6. Why do the authors use descriptive language in the story?

7. What is the story's main idea?

8. How do the authors support the main idea? Include as many specific details as possible in your response.

9. Why do the authors use the word *kitchens* as the title?

10. What are other possible titles for this selection? Why?

11. What did you learn about the shaping of identity by reading this particular selection?

ANOTHER LOOK AT THE SELECTION

The Flashback

> **FLASHBACK:** A flashback is a device writers use to entertain their readers or to make an incident vivid. A flashback is an intensely vivid image of a past event or the insertion of a past event into a story. A flashback can confuse a reader since it breaks the sense of time in a story, moving it back and forth between past and present rather than keeping events in chronological order.

The authors of this story use a flashback for effect. With your classmates, analyze the use of this device.

1. Locate a flashback; identify the specific lines where you found it.

_____

_____

2. Give specific information about the flashback; tell when and where it takes place and the people it involves.

_____

_____

_____

_____

3. Tell how the flashback differs from the main story line in time, place, and people.

_____

_____

_____

_____

4. Why did the authors include a flashback in the story?

_____

_____

_____

_____

5. Tell whether the flashback made it easier or more difficult to understand and enjoy the story.

_____

_____

_____

_____

6. Is the use of flashbacks limited to literature? Have you seen or heard about a flashback in any other type of media? Explain.

_____

_____

_____

_____

VOCABULARY BUILDING

Descriptive Language

In this selection, the authors use descriptive details and descriptive language to tell about the narrator's experiences. The authors use language in this manner to appeal to your senses—to give you an impression of what the woman felt, saw, heard, and smelled in her California kitchen as well as the kitchens of her family in their native country.

Three of the authors' descriptive passages appear below. Follow the directions provided to analyze these passages, to strengthen your comprehension of the material, and to understand more fully how descriptive writing affects readers.

Passage 1

Some instinct of the fingertips after years of sorting to feel the rottenness of the bean with a worm in it or a chewed-out side.

a. Circle all the words in Passage 1 that appeal to your senses.

b. To which of your five senses—sight, touch, sound, smell, or taste—do these words appeal?

_____

c. Explain what you see or feel when you read this passage.

_____

_____

_____

d. Tell if you liked the authors' descriptive writing. Did it make it easier or more difficult to understand the story and the main idea?

_____

_____

_____

_____

Passage 2

I see grains of rice settling in a basin on the counter, turning the water milky with rice polish . . .

a. Circle all the words that appeal to your senses.

b. To which of the five senses do these words appeal?

_____

c. In your own words, restate what the authors describe in this passage.

_____

_____

_____

_____

Passage 3

. . . I find a small curved green bunch to rush home, quick, before it ripens, to peel and boil, bathing in the scent of its cooking, bringing the river to flow through my own kitchen now, the river of my place on earth, the green and musty river of my grandmothers, dripping, trickling, tumbling down from the mountain kitchens of my people.

a. Circle the words that appeal to your senses.

b. To which of the five senses do these words appeal?

_____

c. Explain the message the authors attempt to convey in this passage.

_____

_____

_____

_____

d. The word *river* is used three times in Passage. 3 The narrator tells how the river runs through her kitchen and thus suggests that the river is not a body of water but a sign or symbol representing something else. What do you think the river represents?

_____

_____

_____

_____

e. How can you explain and support your answer about the meaning or symbolism of the river?

_____

_____

_____

_____

IN YOUR WORDS

Descriptive Language

Write your own descriptive passages. Use vivid language and details that create sensory images as you complete the following exercises:

1. You have returned to your country for the first time in several years, and you are enjoying a meal of the foods you missed so much during your time away. Describe the experience of enjoying this meal, creating sensory images about how the food tastes and smells.

_____

_____

_____

_____

2. Describe a special place or an item that you treasure.

_____

_____

_____

_____

_____

Read the descriptions you wrote for exercises 1 and 2. Circle all the words that appeal to the senses. Share your work with several classmates. In groups of three or four, make a list of all the sensory words used. Write notes in your course log about the stories and sensory words you want to remember.

SUMMING UP

Share your thoughts about the selection in a group or with the class. What do others think?

1. How did your classmates react to the descriptive language and images in this selection?

What did people with positive reactions have to say? Did anyone find the descriptive language difficult to understand? What particular parts did your classmates cite to support what they said?

2. What did your classmates think about the main character? What contrast did they find between her lifestyle in California and her experiences in her native country?

3. What aspects of the woman's identity were shaped by her experiences in her native country? How has the woman preserved this part of her identity even though she immigrated to the United States?

4. What do you and your classmates know about the concept of identity for people who have lived in more than one country?

DISCOVER WHAT YOU KNOW

1. How do people in your country greet their family and friends on a day-to-day basis when they visit one another or meet at school, at a grocery store, or in town?

2. Is there a difference in the way people in your country greet people they know well and those who are unfamiliar? If so, give some examples of the differences an observer might see.

3. Is kissing a greeting custom in your country? If so, who kisses whom? What kinds of kisses are appropriate? Which are inappropriate?

4. What differences do you find between the greeting customs in your country and those practiced in the United States?

PREVIEWING

Answer the following questions to preview the selection:

1. **a.** What is the title? _____

   b. What do you know about the selection from this title?

   _____

   _____

   c. Does the title interest you? Explain. _____

   _____

2. **a.** Who is the author? _____

   b. What do you know about the author? _____

   c. Why is the author knowledgeable about the topic? _____

   _____

3. a. Where did this selection appear? _____

    b. What do you know about this source? _____

    _____

    c. Who might want to read about this topic? Why? _____

    _____

4. a. Describe the photograph that accompanies this selection.

    _____

    _____

    b. What is the connection between the photograph and the selection's title?

    _____

    _____

5. a. Are there words in bold print? _____ Do you
    understand them? _____ If not, which words are they?

    _____

    _____

    b. What strategies will you use to find the meaning of these words?

    _____

    _____

    _____

6. a. Now quickly read the first and last paragraphs of the article. What is the
    first paragraph about?

    _____

    _____

    b. What is the last paragraph about? _____

    _____

7. What country's kissing customs does the author discuss? _____

_____

_____

8. What do you expect to learn about this custom in the selection?

_____

_____

_____

KISSING CUSTOMS

I returned not long ago from a three-year assignment in Poland, where men kiss the hands of women as a matter of course when they meet. When I first arrived in Warsaw, I did not think this was such a great idea. At the time I thought of myself as a democratic kid from the streets of New York, and the notion of bending over and brushing my lips over the back of a woman's hand

A kiss as a sign and symbol

struck me as offensively **feudal** and hopelessly **effete.** Each time some perfectly fine woman offered me the back of her hand to kiss, **I stammered** my apology, saying something like, "Gosh, no offense intended, but where I come from we don't carry on like this, and while I respect you enormously, can't we make do with a simple handshake?". . .

But then I began to realize that the Polish custom had one particularly subtle and attractive aspect. After 40 years of living under an unpopular

Communist Government that sought to restrict society to the **proletarian** standard of some **concocted** Soviet model, the Poles were defending themselves with chivalrous customs. Instead of addressing each other with terms like "comrade citizen," as their Government had once urged them to do, Poles **intuitively** responded by assuming the manners of dukes and barons. In such circumstances it was pleasant and instructive to watch factory workers, mailmen, soldiers, peasants and high-school students kiss the hands held out to them while the Communist Party people, often identifiable by their wide ties and out-of-date suits, maintained stiff though **ideologically** correct postures.

Under this kind of social pressure, I kissed. At first it was tricky. There was nothing in my Upper West Side of Manhattan public-school education that prepared me for the act. I had to experiment. I think my first attempts were perhaps too noisy. They may also have been too moist. I realized that generally what I was expected to communicate was respect and not **ardor,** but I didn't want to appear too distant. I had observed some aristocrats take the hands extended to them and swoosh down without making real contact. I was trying for slightly more commitment.

Eventually, I got it right. And, to my surprise, I liked it. Each new encounter became a challenge. I found I needed to make **subtle** little **alterations** in technique as the situations demanded. For instance, if the woman was younger, I would bring her hand to my lips. If she was older, I would bring my lips to her hand. When I could not tell if she was younger or older, I went on the premise that she was younger. Sometimes you could play out little dramas. It was nothing serious or marriage-threatening, but you could, by kissing with more than normal pressure, make yourself noticed—and you could notice yourself being noticed. Or you could imagine you were somebody else, which, at least in my case, can be pleasant.

The real advantage of hand-kissing, I came to realize, was that it provided a ritual that enriched the routine of everyday life. Whenever I returned to the West on holidays I was struck by how few such rituals existed in my own society. Hardly anyone shook hands, let alone kissed them. Instead, waiters would tell me their names before taking my order and wish me a good day as they took my money. But I never felt they really cared. . . .

In this cultural context, I doubt that the United States is ready for hand-kissing. We seem to lack the self-discipline, or perhaps the confidence. . . .

Michael T. Kaufman

GLOSSARY

alteration (n.) a change or modification

ardor (n.) fiery intensity of feeling; strong feeling

concoct (v.) to devise, using skill and intelligence; to create

effete (adj.) worn-out

feudal (adj.) of, relating to, or characteristic of a political and economic system of Europe from the 9th to about the 15th century

ideologically (adv.) concerned with ideas

intuitively (adj.) through senses or perception rather than judgment

proletarian (adj.) of, relating to, or characteristic of the poorest class of working people

stammer (v.) to speak with involuntary pauses or repetitions

subtle (adj.) so slight as to be difficult to detect or analyze

QUICK COMPREHENSION CHECK ☑

Complete the sentences in the following summary paragraph. This time, use your own words to express specific and accurate information from the selection.

Michael T. Kaufman is an American journalist who was on a **(1)** _____ year assignment in **(2)** _____. Mr. Kaufman identifies himself as **(3)** _____.

He mentions his identity because he believes it interfered with his ability to participate in a certain custom practiced in Poland. This particular custom obligated men to kiss **(4)** _____.

Mr. Kaufman did not practice the custom at first, giving the following excuse:

(5) _____.

Eventually, he followed the custom, and his first reaction was **(6)** _____

_____.

His early kisses were not perfect, he claimed, because they were **(7)** _____

_____

and _____.

Eventually, Mr. Kaufman developed an art for performing the custom. The
type of kisses he gave were influenced by a woman's age; for example, he

(8) _____

_____.

Mr. Kaufman analyzes the kissing custom in Poland, relating it to that country's
history and identity. Basically, he claims people in Poland follow this kissing
custom because **(9)** _____.

QUESTIONS FOR THOUGHT AND DISCUSSION

1. Describe the specific custom Kaufman writes about in this selection.

2. Summarize and react to his explanation about why this custom is practiced
in Poland.

3. Explain the connection between customs and identity; support your
statements with examples about yourself or someone you know.

4. Does Michael Kaufman find the kissing custom in Poland compatible or
incompatible with the identity of people in the United States? Explain your
answer.

5. Think of the section where Kaufman describes his first attempts to practice
the kissing custom. In your own words, summarize some of what he says and
describe how it affected you as a reader.

6. Tell about times when you felt uncomfortable about a custom practiced in the
United States.

7. Tell as much as you can about Michael Kaufman's identity based on what
you read in this selection.

8. Identify some customs and practices that tell about your identity. Be specific
about each custom and its message about you.

9. Michael Kaufman suggests that people's identities can change in a new setting.

Reflect on this idea. You left your country and came to the United States. Did
this affect your identity? Explain your answer.

ANOTHER LOOK AT THE SELECTION

Subordinating Conjunctions

A. The author uses another type of connecting word in the following sentences. Read these sentences carefully and answer the question.

   1. When I first arrived in Warsaw, I did not think this [kissing the hands of women] was such a great idea.

   2. If she [the woman] was older, I would bring my lips to her hand.

   3. When I could not tell if she was younger or older, I went on the premise that she was younger.

What connecting words does the author use? _____

SUBORDINATING CONJUNCTION: The type of connecting word the author uses is a **subordinating conjunction.** Subordinating conjunctions connect two or more thoughts in a sentence to improve the flow of writing and to strengthen the meaningful relationship between the thoughts.

These are some of the words that can serve as subordinating conjunctions: *when, since, while, if, once, because, although.*

TIP: When a subordinating conjunction starts a sentence, a comma is needed at the end of the first clause. If the subordinating conjunction is in the sentence between the two clauses, no comma is needed.

Example: When I visit my country, I will see my grandmother.
           I will see my grandmother when I visit my country.

An important note: A subordinating conjunction with one subject and verb is a **sentence fragment,** a sentence structure error in which an incomplete thought is incorrectly punctuated as a sentence.

Example: When I visit my country.

B. Write two sentences of your own about Michael Kaufman's experience in Poland. Use subordinating conjunctions to link ideas in your sentences; circle your connecting words.

   1. _____

   _____

   2. _____

   _____

VOCABULARY BUILDING

Word Analysis

What does the word *identity* mean? What topics do you talk about when you discuss the word *identity*? Find clear and concrete ways for discussing the word by completing the following diagram. Note that *gender*, *age*, *ethnicity*, *role*, and *outlook* are listed as components of *identity*, and examples for these components have been entered as well. Working with a partner or in a group, add more components and examples to the diagram.

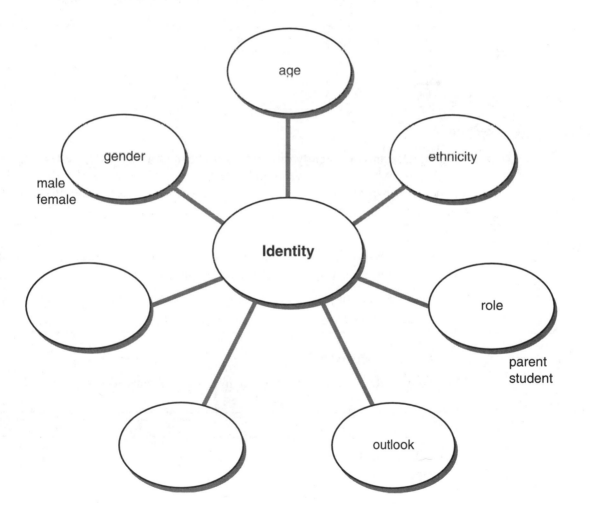

VOCABULARY STRATEGY: *Identity* is an abstract word; it is not an object that you defined through description. Rather, you defined the word by breaking it down into understandable parts and providing examples and details to illustrate these parts.

What other abstract words do you know? Here are some that are probably common in your vocabulary: *success*, *freedom*, *truth*, *independence*, *love*, and *friendship*. Practice defining abstract words by analyzing two of the words listed above. In your course log, draw diagrams for the two words and analyze them using the method you used for *identity*.

IN YOUR WORDS

Explaining Connections

"Kissing Customs" is slightly different from the other two reading selections in this chapter. Whereas the material in Selections 1 and 2 was directly connected to identity, the chapter's topic, the connection between Selection 3 and this topic is more subtle. The exercises in this section will guide you to explore the fit between "Kissing Customs" and identity in a systematic way.

Practice identifying topics, and then, with certainty about the topics, describe, in your words, how Selection 3 relates to the chapter's central point.

1. Circle the word or phrase that represents this chapter's topic:

   life experiences   identity

   family   important places

   customs around the world

2. Based on your work so far, explain this chapter's main idea.

   _____

   _____

3. Explain how "My Father's Black Pride" or "Kitchens" is related to the chapter's topic.

   _____

   _____

   _____

4. Now consider "Kissing Customs" and circle the phrase that best identifies its subject matter:

people in Poland people's identity

unique American customs customs and culture

being a journalist

5. Tell what you learned about identity from this selection. Focus on how the things people do tell about their identity.

_____

_____

6. Support your statement for number 5. Give one example of how Michael Kaufman, people in Poland, or people in the United States follow certain customs.

_____

_____

_____

7. Summarize how "Kissing Customs" is related to the chapter's topic.

_____

_____

_____

8. Make several statements about your identity, as it is shown by the customs you choose to follow and the customs you question.

_____

_____

_____

_____

SUMMING UP

Share your thoughts about the selection in a group or with the class. What do others think?

1. Did your classmates accept Kaufman's explanation about why men in Poland kiss the hands of women when they greet them? If so, restate the reasons he gave. If not, summarize the objections your classmates raised.

2. What did your classmates have to say about the experience of feeling uncomfortable with the customs of another country? What is the source of this discomfort? How does a person cope with the discomfort?

3. Tell whether anyone found humor in this selection. If so, give the location of the humorous sections and restate these parts in your own words. Explain why they are humorous.

4. What did your classmates have to say about the relationship between customs and identity?

5. What did your classmates have to say about the shaping of an immigrant's identity?

CLOSING THE CHAPTER

Take a moment to think about the selections in this chapter and how ideas in them relate to your life. While the topic of identity is fresh in your mind, write a brief paragraph about your identity. Summarize who you are, or write about an experience or event that influenced your developing identity.

REFLECTING AND SYNTHESIZING

1. Connect the different ideas in the chapter. Write a paragraph on the many factors that can shape an individual's identity.

2. Freewrite on one or more of the following topics:

   your most treasured possession

   your favorite place

   special people in your life

   your favorite food

   your hobbies or interests

   a typical person from your country

   a typical American

   a time when your identity was challenged

   a custom that tells about you or someone you know

   a belief that tells about you or someone you know

2

PATHWAYS AND PASSAGES:
EXPLORING OUR HUMAN STORIES

OPENING THOUGHT

There are only two or three human stories,
and they go on repeating themselves
as fiercely as if they never happened before.

Willa Cather, *O Pioneers!* (1913)

Think about the chapter's title, quotation, and opening photograph. Answer the following questions:

1. Restate the quotation in your own words.

_____

_____

_____

2. Explain whether you agree or disagree with the quotation's message.

_____

_____

_____

3. List the stages of a typical "human story." Then tell how the path of life can be different for a particular group of people—for example, children, teens, young adults, or the elderly.

_____

_____

_____

_____

_____

_____

4. What circumstances might cause the stories of people's lives to differ?

_____

_____

_____

_____

5. Tell whether your answer to question 4 supports or argues against the chapter's quotation.

_____

_____

_____

_____

Share your thoughts with your partner, group, or class.

The selections in this chapter describe some of the major life decisions or events people have experienced. Think about human stories—the stories of people's lives—the events that shape them, and whether people's basic human stories are the same or different. As you read the selections, write your thoughts about them and the words you need to study further in your course log.

Selection 1

DISCOVER WHAT YOU KNOW

1. Tell about a time when you had to make an important decision.

2. What factors did you take into consideration when making this decision?

3. Who helped you make this decision?

4. What was the outcome of the decision you made?

PREVIEWING

> **TIPS FOR DEVELOPING PREVIEWING SKILLS:** The concept of previewing is the same for all types of reading material. However, the specific questions you ask when you preview will vary according to a selection's unique features, such as its photographs, tables, graphics, special format, layout, and so on. Notice how the preview questions in this chapter differ slightly from selection to selection.
>
> In the remaining chapters, you will preview selections on your own, without a list of questions to guide you. Prepare for this work by studying the questions below. Take notes in your course log about the structure and purpose of previewing questions. Add to these notes every time you preview a selection in the chapter. Tell how and why previewing questions differ from selection to selection.

Answer the following questions to preview the selection:

1. **a.** What is the title?

   _____

   b. What is the possible connection between this selection's title and the chapter's title?

   _____

   _____

2. **a.** Describe the photograph that accompanies the selection.

   _____

   _____

   _____

   b. How does this photograph relate to the chapter's title?

   _____

   _____

   _____

3. a. How does the form of this selection differ from the form of the selections you have read so far?

_____

_____

b. What is your experience with this type of reading material?

_____

_____

4. a. Who is the poet?

_____

b. What do you know about this poet?

_____

_____

5. a. Are there any words in bold print? _____ Do you understand them? _____ If not, which words are they? _____

_____

b. What do you think these words mean?

_____

_____

6. a. Now quickly read the first and last sections of the selection. What is the first section about?

_____

_____

b. What is the last section about?

_____

_____

7. What questions do you have now that you have previewed the selection?

_____

_____

_____

8. What do you expect to read about in this selection?

_____

_____

_____

THE ROAD NOT TAKEN

Two roads **diverged** in a yellow wood,
And sorry I could not travel both
And be one traveler, long I stood
And looked down one as far as I could
5   To where it bent in the **undergrowth**;

Then took the other, as just as fair,
And having perhaps the better claim,
Because it was grassy and wanted wear;
Though as for that the passing there
10 Had worn them really about the same,

And both that morning equally lay
In leaves no step had **trodden** black.
Oh, I kept the first for another day!
Yet knowing how way leads on to way,
15 I doubted if I should ever come back.

I shall be telling this with a **sigh**
Somewhere ages and ages **hence**:
Two roads diverged in a wood, and I—
I took the one less traveled by,
20 And that has made all the difference.

Two paths to follow

From THE POETRY OF ROBERT FROST edited by Edward Connery Lathem, © 1969 by
    Henry Holt and Co. Reprinted by permission of Henry Holt & Co., LLC.

GLOSSARY

diverge (v.) to go or extend in different directions from a common point; to branch out

undergrowth (n.) low-growing plants, small trees, and shrubs beneath the trees in a forest

trodden (v.) past participle of **to tread,** to walk on, over, or along

sigh (n.) the act of exhaling audibly in a long, deep breath, as in weariness or relief

hence (adv.) for this reason; from this source; from this time

QUICK COMPREHENSION CHECK ☑

Complete the sentences in this brief summary about the selection:

The narrator tells about a time when he was walking through (1) _____

_____. He describes two roads that (2) _____

_____. Before deciding which road to follow,

he (3) _____. Then he made his decision. He

chose not to follow the (4) _____, thinking he

might never (5) _____. Rather he took the

(6) _____, the one less (7) _____.

QUESTIONS FOR THOUGHT AND DISCUSSION

1. During what season of the year is this poem set? How can you tell?

2. How old do you think the narrator is?

3. What might the wood and the roads symbolize?

4. Tell how the two roads differ from one another.

5. What images do you see in this poem? How do these affect you?

6. How does the narrator determine which road to follow?

7. What impact does the narrator's decision have?

8. What general message does Frost wish to convey in this poem?

9. Discuss the meaning of the poem's title.

10. Discuss the significance of this title.

11. Tell about a time when you followed a road less traveled.

ANOTHER LOOK AT THE SELECTION

Rhyming Words

A. Like many poems, this selection contains rhyming words. Find the different sets of rhyming words in "The Road Not Taken" and list them in the following sections:

Set 1

_____

_____

_____

_____

Set 2

_____

_____

_____

_____

Set 3

_____

_____

_____

_____

Set 4

_____

_____

_____

_____

Set 5

_____

_____

_____

_____

Set 6

_____

_____

_____

_____

Set 7   **Set 8**

_____   _____

_____   _____

_____   _____

_____   _____

B. With a partner or in a group, do the following:

    1. In the blank lines in Part A, write in other words that rhyme with those listed.

    2. Recite all the words listed to be sure that you are pronouncing them correctly and that your rhyming sounds are consistent.

C. With a partner or in a group, develop a new list of rhyming words and practice pronunciation once again.

    a. _____

    b. _____

    c. _____

    d. _____

D. Now, on your own, write a verse of at least six lines in which some or all of the words rhyme. Write your verse about a topic or photograph of your choice.

_____

_____

_____

_____

_____

_____

E. Share what you wrote with a partner, in a group, or in general class discussion.

VOCABULARY BUILDING

Literary Terms

Poetry is one of many literary forms. Many specialized terms are important in discussions about poetry.

A. In the following spaces, list any literary terms you know from your study of literature in other courses or from your personal reading:

1. _____

2. _____

3. _____

4. _____

5. _____

B. Write the letter of the definition in the blank beside the correct literary term.

Literary Terms	Definitions
_____ **1.** verse	**a.** the time, place, or circumstances in which a literary work takes place
_____ **2.** stanza	**b.** the use of vivid, figurative language to represent objects, actions, or ideas
_____ **3.** symbol	**c.** one line of poetry or a subdivision of a long poem
_____ **4.** rhyme	**d** a word or phrase that represents a particular idea, concept, or object
_____ **5.** narrator	**e.** a section of a poem, composed of two or more lines
_____ **6.** imagery	**f.** corresponding end sounds of words or of lines of verse
_____ **7.** rhythm	**g.** person who tells a story
_____ **8.** setting	**h.** patterned movement regulated by accented and unaccented syllables

VOCABULARY STRATEGY: You used a content-based approach for this study of literary terms. The words are related to one another in one subject: literature. A content approach to vocabulary development is a sensible approach. It focuses on the context in which the vocabulary words will actually be used. When you study vocabulary with the intention of understanding and using words rather than just memorizing them, you are likely to remember the words and use them correctly.

C. Think about the content approach to vocabulary development. Can you think of an academic subject you find difficult because you need to develop your vocabulary in the area? What words in this subject area give you difficulty? In your course log, write about this academic subject and the vocabulary you need to learn. Study the relationships among the words in your list. Examine the words in your textbook and try to find meaning through context; use a dictionary to find a formal definition. Use the words actively when you think about or discuss the course. Make these words part of your vocabulary.

IN YOUR WORDS

Interpreting Poetry

In the Quick Comprehension Check, you completed a summary of the poem's literal meaning. The paragraph retells what the author stated; it does not explore the moral or meaning that is suggested by what the words symbolize.

In this section, develop and write your interpretation of the poem. Think about the *wood* and the different *roads* the author writes about. What concepts, situations, or events in life could these words represent?

Write what you believe to be the poem's meaning or message:

_____

_____

_____

_____

_____

_____

_____

_____

_____

_____

SUMMING UP

Share your thoughts about the selection in a group or with the class. What do others think?

1. What did the group know about the study of poetry?

2. Did everyone agree on the poem's meaning? If so, tell how the group summarized the poem. If not, identify points of disagreement.

3. How did the group react to the study of poetry?

Selection 2

DISCOVER WHAT YOU THINK

1. At what age are young people capable of making their own decisions?

2. What decisions, if any, are young adults capable of making?

3. Should parents play a significant role in their children's decisions about critical life passages such as education, marriage, and moving away from home? Give reasons for your response.

PREVIEWING

Answer the following questions to preview the selection:

1. **a.** What is the title? _____

   b. What information do you have about this title?

   _____

   _____

   c. What information do you need?

   _____

   _____

2. **a.** Who is the author? _____

   b. What do you know about the author?

   _____

   _____

3. **a.** Describe the illustration that accompanies the selection.

   _____

   _____

   b. What is the possible connection between the illustration and the selection?

   _____

   _____

4. **a.** Are there any words in darker, or bold, print? _____ Do you understand them? _____ If not, which words are they?

   _____

   _____

   b. What do you think these words mean?

   _____

   _____

5. **a.** Quickly read the first and last paragraphs of the selection. What is the first paragraph about?

   _____

   _____

   b. What is the last paragraph about?

   _____

   _____

6. Tell what you know so far about the characters in the story.

_____

_____

_____

7. What questions do you have after previewing the selection?

_____

_____

_____

8. What do you expect to read about in this selection?

_____

_____

_____

from *CANTORA*

Her hair still damp and braided with ribbons, Rosario, wearing a clean white dress, hurried to the other side of the **hacienda** and her father's study. As she approached the big double-oak doors, she slowed her pace, stopping with her hands on the iron handles. She took a deep breath to **compose** herself, as her mother had taught her, and then quietly entered her father's study.

"Good day, Papá," Rosario said formally.

Ramón Carras stood behind his desk looking out of the window. Rosario waited. She didn't move or **fidget.** Her mother had taught her well. Finally, her father turned to her and held out his right hand. Rosario moved forward and around the desk and bent to take her father's hand. She kissed the back of it as he held it out to her.

"Good evening, Rosario. Where have you been? You are late, my daughter."

"Yes, Papá. I was playing by the river. I forgot the time. Can you forgive me, Papá?"

"Today, I would forgive you anything, Rosario."

Curious, she asked, "What is so special about today, Papá?"

"Today we must talk about your future."

20 "What do you mean, my future?"

"The future I have chosen for you. The future I chose for you the day you were born. For me and your mamá, it was the happiest day on this **hacienda.** Did you know, there was a fiesta that lasted three days? We all celebrated, the family, the servants, even the **caballeros.**"

25 Almost in a whisper, Rosario answered, "No, Papá. I did not know."

"On that day," he continued, "I decided your future. It is a very good future, one that will **ensure** you are cared for and loved all of your days. Your sons will be **heirs** to both my **estate** and to the **estate** of your new family, the Alcanzars."

30 "Who are the Alcanzars, Papá?"

"Antonio Alcanzar is my childhood friend. He lived on the **adjoining** estate next to my father's in Spain. We played together, rode our ponies together, went to school together."

"In Spain, Papá?"

35 "Yes, Antonio and his family are still in Barcelona. He has a son, Frederico. He is seventeen, now. A fine young man, Antonio writes that

Frederico **excels** in school and will attend the university next year. Frederico is to be your husband, Rosario."

40 She did not move. Instead, she stood in front of her father and watched him turn away from the window to sit in his chair. He was next to her now, his eyes on her. She stared out the window, reaching for a peace she felt she would never know again. The sky was beginning to lose its blinding brilliance. Today, the light had spilled over her and Alejandro in the foothills. Everything they had touched seemed to have been bathed in this

45 light. Now, it was fading slowly as her father watched her.

Fighting to maintain her control, she said, "Papá, what are you saying to me?"

"I am saying that it is time for you to leave your mother and me. It is time for you to join your new family in Barcelona. You will live with them

50 until you are sixteen, and then you and Frederico will marry. You will be treated with the same love and caring you have received from your mother and me. You will be very precious to them, Rosario. Frederico is also their only child. They never had a daughter, so they look forward to your arrival."

"My arrival? What arrival? Papá, what are you saying?"

55 Panicking now, she turned to him. Where was her mother? Why wasn't she here? She won't allow this, Rosario was certain.

"In three days, you will begin your journey to your new home. Juana will accompany you. She will stay with you in Barcelona. She will always serve you and your children."

60 "Children? What children? Papá, I don't want to get married. Certainly, I don't want to marry a man I do not know!"

"Rosario, this has been decided. There is no one here who would be worthy of marrying you. This is a good and proper arrangement I have made for you, with a family who will love you and understand your needs. There

65 will be no discussion about it. It is decided."

"But, Papá, please listen to me! I do not wish to go to Barcelona! I do not wish to leave you and Mamá! I do not want to marry anyone! Please don't send me away!". . .

"Frederico was four years old when Antonio suggested this **alliance.** I

70 realized it was right for you, so we signed the **contract** when you were three months old."

"A contract, Papá? You signed a contract? Like a business deal? I am one of your business deals?" Abruptly, she pulled away from him. . . .

Excerpt from *Cantora* by Sylvia López-Medina. Copyright © 1992. Originally printed by the University of New Mexico Press. Used with permission.

GLOSSARY

adjoining (adj.) next to or attached to

caballeros **(n.)** horsemen; cowboys

compose (v.) to make calm or tranquil; to settle or adjust

ensure (v.) to make sure or certain

estate (n.) all of one's properties, especially those left after death

excel (v.) to be superior to; to surpass or outdo

fidget (v.) to move nervously or restlessly

hacienda (n.) a large estate in Spanish speaking countries; the main house of such an estate

heir (n.) a person who receives or is entitled to receive the estate, rank, title, or office of another

QUICK COMPREHENSION CHECK ☑

Complete the sentences in this brief summary about the selection:

Rosario was in a hurry as she approached **(1)** _____

_____. She had to stop to **(2)** _____

herself before entering. She greeted her father, who was **(3)** _____

_____ when she entered. Eventually, he turned to

greet her and asked **(4)** _____.

Rosario's father indicated that this day was a special day for her since they were

going to talk about her **(5)** _____. He told

Rosario about a decision he made when she was born, that she would

(6) _____.

Rosario did not move when he said this. She thought about the afternoon and the

time she had spent with **(7)** _____. Then she asked her

father to repeat what he said. Once again, Rosario's father spoke about her future.

He said she was going to travel to **(8)** _____ to be with

the (9) _____ family and would marry their

son (10) _____ when she became

(11) _____. Rosario's father was firm

about this decision even though she said she did not want to leave. Rosario

became more angry when she concluded that her father handled her future like

(12) _____.

QUESTIONS FOR THOUGHT AND DISCUSSION

1. Describe the relationship between Rosario and her father.

2. Why was Rosario's mother not present for the discussion about Rosario's future?

3. Give a detailed account of what Rosario's father planned for her future. When did this planning take place?

4. At one point, Rosario's thoughts turn to someone named Alejandro. Find the section where this person is mentioned and try to explain who he is.

5. What adjectives describe how Rosario felt when her father used the word *contract* in the conversation about her future?

6. Describe the expectations Rosario's parents have for her and examine the possible cultural explanations for these expectations.

7. How does the author portray the following groups: parents, children, boys, and girls?

8. How free is Rosario to shape her own life story?

9. The story closes without final resolution.
How do you think the story ends?
How would you like to see the story end?

10. Should parents play a significant role in their children's decisions about important topics like marriage, work, and finances? Explain your response.

11. How does Rosario's situation as the main character differ from the situation the narrator experiences in "The Road Not Taken"?

ANOTHER LOOK AT THE SELECTION

Direct Questions

Direct questions appear frequently in the exchanges between Rosario and her father. For example, in the fourth paragraph, Ramón Carras asks his daughter, "Where have you been?"

In this section, you will review the direct question as a grammatical structure by doing the following:

1. List words that often serve as the first word of a direct question.

    a. _____   d. _____

    b. _____   e. _____

    c. _____   f. _____

2. Go back to the story and find three other direct questions that Rosario or her father asks. Write the direct questions you found on the following lines:

    a. _____

    _____

    b. _____

    _____

    c. _____

    _____

3. Circle and label the subjects and their verbs in the direct questions you wrote.

4. Go back to the story and find three statements that Rosario or her father makes.

5. Write those statements on the following lines:

    a. _____

    _____

    b. _____

    _____

    c. _____

    _____

6. Circle and label the subjects and their verbs in the preceding statements.

7. In the following space, explain how direct questions and statements differ in structure. Tell all the differences you see. Be sure to tell about the order and placement of subjects and their verbs.

_____

_____

_____

_____

8. Practice your knowledge about sentence structure by writing six sentences in the space below. The first three sentences should be statements in which you retell information from *Cantora*. The other three should be direct questions that probe what you would like to know about the story or its characters.

Statements: Tell what happened in the story.

a. _____

_____

b. _____

_____

c. _____

Direct Questions: Ask about a character's feelings, ask for background information, or ask why certain events took place or why certain circumstances exist.

a. _____

_____

b. _____

_____

c. _____

_____

VOCABULARY BUILDING

Transition Words

A. Following are three different approaches for organizing information. Which of the three best describes how the story from *Cantora* is organized? Circle your answer.

    1. a **spatial** arrangement in which information is presented according to where it is placed or located

    2. a **hierarchical** arrangement in which points of information are presented in order of importance

    3. a **chronological** arrangement in which information is presented in time order

B. Which words in the selection support your answer? List at least three examples here.

    1. _____

    2. _____

    3. _____

C. Use the following table if you need help with the type of words you should be looking for:

RELATIONSHIP AMONG IDEAS	TRANSITIONAL WORDS AND PHRASES
Addition	additionally, also, moreover
Cause/Effect	as a result, consequently, therefore
Clarification	in other words
Contrast	however, in contrast, on the other hand
Emphasis	indeed, in fact
Example	for example, for instance
Sequence	afterwards, at first, eventually, finally, next, previously, second, subsequently, then
Similarity	in the same way, likewise, similarly
Summation	in conclusion, in summary, overall, thus

IN YOUR WORDS

Writing Dialogue

One of the author's strategies for developing the story is dialogue, or conversation. You learn about Rosario and her father and the events in their lives through what they say to one another.

What Rosario and her father say to one another, though, may be very different from the conversations you might have with your parents or your children under similar circumstances.

Study one particular exchange between Rosario and her father and then write a new dialogue for the situation they discuss. The dialogue you create will illustrate your way of speaking to your parents or children and the way you would handle discussion about a topic in the selection.

To complete the exercise, do the following:

1. Scan the selection carefully to find an exchange between Rosario and her father that you would like to re-create.

2. Copy this exchange.

_____

_____

_____

_____

_____

_____

_____

_____

_____

_____

3. Study the exchange and consider how you would change both the language and content. Write notes in the margin about why you want to rewrite the dialogue and how you might state what you wish to say.

4. Now rewrite the dialogue. Feel free to change the names of the speakers, the language they use, the messages they convey, and the values or intentions they express.

_____

_____

_____

_____

_____

_____

_____

_____

_____

_____

_____

_____

5. Look at what you wrote and explain how it differs from the passage you copied for number 2.

_____

_____

_____

_____

_____

SUMMING UP

Share your thoughts about the selection in a group or with the class. What do others think?

1. How did you and your classmates react to what Rosario's father said during their meeting in the study? If reactions differed, explain how and why they did.

2. Summarize what the group said about Rosario's situation as well as cultural factors and the roles of men and women.

3. What did the group have to say about parents' roles in their children's decision making?

Selection 3

DISCOVER WHAT YOU THINK

1. Where is Guatemala?

2. What do you know about the politics and history of the country and surrounding region during the late 1900s until present time?

3. What do you know about the roles of men and women in Guatemala and other countries in Central America?

4. In what ways can the political conditions in a country affect marriage and family life?

5. How can political conditions in a country affect people's attitudes about marriage?

PREVIEWING

Answer the following questions to preview the selection:

1. **a.** What is the title? _____

_____

_____

    b. What is the possible connection between the selection's title and the chapter's title?

_____

_____

_____

2. a. Describe the photograph that accompanies the selection.

_____

_____

_____

    b. How does this photograph relate to the chapter's title?

_____

_____

_____

3. a. Who tells this story? _____

_____

    b. What do you know about this person?

_____

_____

_____

4. Who might be interested in reading this story? Why?

_____

_____

_____

5. **a.** Are there any words in darker, or bold, print? _____ Do you understand them? _____ If not, which ones are they? _____

_____

b. What do you think these words might mean?

_____

_____

6. **a.** Quickly read the first and last paragraphs of this selection. What is the first paragraph about?

_____

_____

b. What is the last paragraph about?

_____

_____

7. What questions do you have after previewing the selection?

_____

_____

_____

_____

8. What do you expect to read about in this selection?

_____

_____

_____

_____

_____

WOMEN AND POLITICAL COMMITMENT: RIGOBERTA RENOUNCES MARRIAGE AND MOTHERHOOD

from *I, RIGOBERTA MENCHÚ*
AN INDIAN WOMAN IN GUATEMALA

I still haven't approached the subject—and it's perhaps a very long subject—of women in Guatemala. We have to put them into categories, anyway: working-class women, peasant women, poor ***ladino*** women, and **bourgeois** women, middle-class women. There is something important about women in Guatemala, especially Indian women, and that something is her relationship with the earth—between earth and the mother. The earth gives food and the woman gives life. Because of this closeness the woman must keep this respect for the earth as a secret of her own. The relationship between the mother and the earth is like the relationship between husband and wife. There is a constant dialogue between the earth and the woman. This feeling is born in women because of the responsibilities they have, which men do not have.

That is how I've been able to analyse my specific task in the organisation. I realize that many ***compañeros***, who are revolutionaries and good *compañeros*, never lose the feeling that their views are better than those of any women in charge of them. Of course, we mustn't dismiss the great value of those *compañeros*, but we can't let them do just whatever they like. I have a responsibility, I am in charge, and they must accept me for what I am. But in this respect I've met serious problems when handing out tasks to those *compañeros*, and I've often found it upsetting having to assume this role. . . . I found all this very difficult and, as I was saying, I came up against revolutionary *compañeros*, *compañeros* who had many ideas about making a revolution, but who had trouble accepting that a woman could participate in the struggle not only in **superficial** things but in **fundamental** things. I've also had to punish many *compañeros* who try to prevent their women taking part in the struggle or carrying out any task. They're sometimes willing to let them

Women involved in the people's struggle.

35 participate but only within certain limits. They start saying: 'Oh no, not that. No, not here. No.' Well, we've had to talk seriously with these *compañeros* to solve that problem. . . .

40 The situation we are in means that our women don't get married because they're expecting something happy, a lovely family, pleasure, or something different from what they already have. No, not at all. They know that a very hard life awaits them. Although for us marriage is something joyful (because the concept our ancestors had was that our race must not die out and we must follow our traditions and customs as they did), at the same time it is something very painful, knowing that when you get married you'll have the **45** responsibility of bringing up your children, and not only of looking after them, but worrying, trying to make do, and hoping they live. In Guatemala, it's unusual for a family not to see some of their young children die.

Well, in my case, I analysed my ideas for not getting married with some of my *compañeros*. I realized that what I said wasn't crazy, that it wasn't **50** some personal mad idea, but that our whole situation makes women think very hard before getting married, because who will look after the children, who will feed them? . . . I thought I was alone in feeling like this, but when I discussed it with other women, they saw the whole thing of getting married in the same way I did. It is terrible to know that such a hard life awaits you, **55** with so much responsibility to make sure your children live. You can't think any other way in Guatemala: when you get engaged or married, you immediately think of the many children you are going to have. I've been in love many times but it was precisely because of that fear that I didn't jump into marriage. But the time came when I saw clearly—it was actually when **60** I'd begun my life as a revolutionary—that I was fighting for a people and for many children who hadn't had anything to eat. . . .

And then when my parents died, I felt what a daughter feels for a father and mother when they die, and even more so because of the way they died. That's when I decided, although I can't say that it's a final decision because I **65** am open to life. My idea is, though, that there will be time enough after our victory; but at the moment I wouldn't feel happy having a *compañero* and giving myself to him while so many of our people are not thinking of their own personal happiness and haven't a single moment to rest.

The conclusion I came to was that, while we have so many problems, we **70** shouldn't look for more. There are married women in the struggle, however, who contribute as much as I do, **compañeras** who have five or six children and do magnificent work. Being afraid of all that is a certain trauma I have. I'm even more afraid when I think that if I had a *compañero*, I'd probably love him very much and I wouldn't want it to be for only a week or two **75** because after that he wouldn't be there. While I don't have this problem, I won't look for it. But, as I said, I'm open to life. It doesn't mean that I reject everything because I know that things come in their time and when you do things calmly, they work much better.

As I said, I was engaged once. At one time he wanted a lot of things in
80 life; a nice house for his children and a peaceful life. But I didn't think like that. We'd known each other since we were children, but unfortunately he left our village and had to go to the city. He became a factory worker, and then really turned into a *compañero* with good work **prospects** who thought differently from the way I and my village thought. So, when I became a
85 revolutionary I had to choose between two things—the struggle or my *compañero*. . . . Well, there I was between these two things—choosing him or my people's struggle. And that's what I chose, and I left my *compañero* with much sadness and a heavy heart. But I told myself that I had a lot to do for my people and I didn't need a pretty house while they lived in **horrific**
90 conditions like those I had been born and grew up in. Well, that's when we went our separate ways. I told him that it wasn't right for me to stay with him because he had other ideas and we'd never understand each other, since he wanted one thing and I'd always go on wanting another. Then I went on with our struggle and now I'm on my own. But, as I said, there'll be a time
95 when things will be different, when we'll all be happy, perhaps not with nice houses, but at least we won't see our lands running with blood and sweat.

I, Rigoberta Menchú: An Indian Woman in Guatemala. Edited by Elisabeth Burgos-Debray, translated by Ann Wright (London: Verso). Reprinted with permission.

This selection is written in British English.

GLOSSARY

bourgeois (n.) one belonging to the middle class

compañera **(n.)** female companion or friend

compañero **(n.)** male companion or friend

fundamental (adj.) basic; elementary

horrific (adj.) terrifying

ladino **(n.)** middle class

prospect (n.) chances, especially of success

revolutionary (n.) one who supports or engages in an effort to bring about radical change

superficial (adj.) obvious and unimportant

QUICK COMPREHENSION CHECK ☑

Complete the sentences of this brief summary paragraph of the selection's content:

Rigoberta Menchú says that women in Guatemala have an important relationship, a relationship between **(1)** _____ and the **(2)** _____. Aware of this relationship and what it suggests about the role of women, Rigoberta has analyzed her work and the important decisions she must make. She thinks about the men who feel their views are **(3)** _____. She also describes men who cannot accept a woman who **(4)** _____ _____. Because of the situation with men and because of conditions in the country, women in Guatemala, like Rigoberta, are concerned about getting **(5)** _____. There is a certain pain associated with marriage; when women in Guatemala get married, they know they must worry about **(6)** _____. Rigoberta discussed her fear of getting married with other women, and she learned **(7)** _____. Eventually, Rigoberta had to make her personal decision about marriage. She had to choose between **(8)** _____ and **(9)** _____. She chose **(10)** _____ although she does say there may be a time when **(11)** _____.

QUESTIONS FOR THOUGHT AND DISCUSSION

1. Rigoberta discusses a relationship that is important to women in Guatemala. What is this important relationship? What does it say about the role of women in the country?

2. According to Rigoberta, how do men in Guatemala regard women? How do the men react to women's opinions? How do the men feel about women participating in the country's political struggle?

3. What is Rigoberta's work?

4. How do men's views of women affect Rigoberta's ability to do her work?

5. How does Rigoberta describe the responsibilities of marriage, especially the responsibilities for women in Guatemala?

6. What did Rigoberta learn when she discussed marriage with her friends?

7. How does Rigoberta feel about getting married? What painful personal experience intensified this view?

8. What choice did Rigoberta have to make? What was her decision? Why?

9. What do you think about Rigoberta's decision?

10. Will Rigoberta ever change her mind about getting married?

ANOTHER LOOK AT THE SELECTION

Spoken Language

Rigoberta's story was recorded in an interview and then translated into English. It, therefore, offers the reader an example of spoken language. Examine and react to the structure and effect of spoken language by completing the following:

1. List five sentences or expressions from the selection which show that Rigoberta told her story to another person.

   a. _____

   b. _____

   c. _____

   d. _____

   e. _____

2. How did this style of storytelling affect your comprehension of the material? Why?

   _____

   _____

   _____

   _____

3. What effect, if any, did this style of storytelling have on your interest in the material? Why?

_____

_____

_____

4. Study the differences between spoken language and written language.

a. Work with a classmate. One of you will be the speaker; the other will be the recorder. The speaker should tell a very short story (three to four sentences) about himself or herself. The story can be a statement about identity, a statement about interests and hobbies, a statement of background information, or a statement about personal goals. The listener will record exactly what the speaker says in the following space.

_____

_____

_____

_____

b. Continue to work with your classmate. Rewrite the previous information. Replace the pronoun *I* with the person's name and continue to revise the material so that you are writing about the person rather than retelling what he or she said.

_____

_____

c. Look at the two passages together and discuss the ways in which they differ. List at least three of the differences here. Focus on specific evidence, such as pronouns and verb forms.

_____

_____

_____

_____

VOCABULARY BUILDING

The Language of the Revolutionary

> **revolution (n.)** the overthrow of one government and its replacement with
> another; a sudden or momentous change in a situation

Rigoberta identifies herself as a revolutionary. Complete the sentence below to
define what Rigoberta does.

A revolutionary like Rigoberta Menchú is someone who _____

_____

_____

1. What rights do revolutionaries fight for when they try to bring about change?
   Using your knowledge of other revolutions in world history—those you have
   read about and those you or your family may have experienced—list some of
   the rights for which revolutionaries fight. Two examples are provided.

   justice _____

   freedom of religion _____

   _____

   _____

   _____

   _____

   _____

   _____

   _____

2. Often, after a revolution takes place, the rights people fought for are recorded in some type of legal document. Are you familiar with any such document? If so, what is this document and what does it say?

_____

_____

_____

_____

_____

3. Many organizations and governments produce a *Statement of Rights* like the one you just discussed. The United Nations, for example, has documents about the rights of women, children, and people of different cultures. The government of the United States has developed similar documents on a number of topics, such as the elderly, immigrants, and veterans. Focus your thinking about the language of the revolutionary by writing your own *Statement of Rights* for a specific group of people. Select any one of the groups mentioned here or a group of your own choice and write a statement about the basic human rights this particular group of people should be entitled to.

_____

_____

_____

_____

_____

Read your *Statement of Rights* aloud in class.

IN YOUR WORDS

The Conditions in Guatemala

Read the final sentence of the selection. In this sentence Rigoberta Menchú makes her most vivid statement about the conditions in her country. Someday, she says, "we won't see our lands running with blood and sweat." In other sections, Rigoberta hints about or provides additional detail about life in Guatemala. Review the selection once again, looking for references to life in Guatemala and then do the following:

1. Write a summary of the conditions Rigoberta has experienced and has struggled to change.

_____

_____

_____

_____

_____

2. Have you, someone in your family, or someone you know experienced conditions like those in Guatemala? Where? When? How did you, your family member, or the person you know react to the situation?

_____

_____

_____

_____

3. Would you ever be able to fight against the government as Rigoberta has? Why?

_____

_____

_____

_____

4. Is Rigoberta's work as a revolutionary for her own personal interest or for the interest of others? How do you know what her intentions are? Where do you find support for your answer in the selection?

_____

_____

_____

_____

_____

SUMMING UP

Share your thoughts about the selection in a group or with the class. What do others think?

1. How did everyone react to Rigoberta's decision about marriage? Did everyone accept the reasons Rigoberta gave to support her choice?

2. What did the group say about Rigoberta's work as a revolutionary? Did they believe her actions were based on self interest or on the interests of others? If disagreement existed, summarize the different viewpoints and their supporting reasons.

3. What different _Statements of Rights_ did your classmates develop? In what ways do these statements differ? In what ways are they similar?

4. What are the fundamental human rights to which all people are entitled, regardless of their ethnic background, religion, gender, and age?

Selection 4

DISCOVER WHAT YOU KNOW

1. What educational goals do many young immigrants in the United States have? Why?

2. What obstacles may interfere with these educational goals?

3. Who can guide immigrants who want to pursue an education?

4. Tell about the people you know who have reached their educational goals in spite of obstacles.

5. What are the benefits of getting a college education?

PREVIEWING

1. **a.** What is the title? _____

   b. What does this title mean? _____

   _____

2. **a.** Describe the photograph that accompanies the article.

   _____

   _____

   b. Tell whether the young people in the photograph look like people you know.

   _____

   _____

3. **a.** What is the source for this article? _____

   b. Who would read this article? _____

   c. Why? _____

4. **a.** Who is the author? _____

   b. Why did he write this article? _____

   _____

5. Are there any words in bold print? _____ Do you understand them? _____ If not, what strategies will you use for learning about these words?

_____

_____

6. a. Quickly read the first and last paragraphs of the selection. What is the first paragraph about?

_____

_____

_____

b. What is the last paragraph about?

_____

_____

7. What questions do you have after previewing the selection?

_____

_____

_____

_____

8. What do you expect to read about in this selection?

_____

_____

_____

_____

SIX WHOSE PATH TO EXCELLENCE WAS ON THE MEAN STREETS OF ADVERSITY

It is no small **feat** to earn a 95 average at the Humanities Preparatory Academy in Greenwich Village and to graduate at the top of a class of 158. It is almost unheard of to pull it off in two years.

It certainly does not help if, like 18-year-old Elizabeth Murray, you did your homework in the littered Bronx hallways and stairwells where you usually slept because your mother had died of AIDS and your drug-addicted father was suffering from the same disease.

Across town, in Elmhurst, Queens, QiQi Cheng, 18, attained a 96 average, also squeezing four years of high school into two. When she graduates this June, it will be as **valedictorian.** Yet it was not even three years ago that she stepped off a plane from Shanghai, knowing only a few words of English.

And in Queens Village, LeTicia Williams will graduate with a 90 average, even though she **virtually** dropped out of school for more than two years, spending her days fighting with her drug-addicted mother for money to feed her younger brothers.

The three students are among six who were chosen this week, from a pool of almost 3,000 applicants citywide, to receive the first New York Times College Scholarship Program awards. For some, the scholarships—$12,000 a year for four years—are more than their parents' annual income.

In many respects, the six are a **statistical** snapshot of poor and working-class students in the city. Yet it seems a snapshot that could have been taken almost any time this century: immigrants, children of immigrants, refugees, those who came here from other cities; black, Chinese, Irish-American, Dominican-American; children of porters and factory workers, welfare recipients and waitresses.

What they have in common, however, is that they not only succeeded academically, but also did so by **persevering** in the face of difficult, even **harrowing,** circumstances.

One winner, Mirela Miraj, 18, arrived in New York only three years ago from Albania, where she and her family were **persecuted** because they were Roman Catholics and had once tried to **commandeer** a military boat to escape to Yugoslavia.

Mirela was 10 then, and she lives with the memory of seeing a bullet shatter a window in the ship's hold and strike her 4-year-old niece in the head, killing her.

"I didn't know what to do, I was so young," she recalled this week. "I didn't even know to cry." This summer she will graduate from Grover Cleveland High School in Middle Village, Queens, with a 92 average. She has applied to Columbia University. . . .

LeTicia, 17, recalled being made fun of in school in Cleveland, where she grew up before moving to New York to live with a grandmother, because she interpreted in sign language for her parents, both of whom are deaf, when they came to see her teachers.

Denise De Las Nueces, another winner, overcame not only poverty but extreme shyness that caused her to **stutter.** She forced herself to speak in front of audiences, and even became a lecturer at her local church parish.

Sister Eileen Regina, moderator of the marching band and a Spanish teacher at Cathedral High School on East 56th Street, said yesterday that Denise, 17, often told how she fell in love with science: her father, a doorman, brought her astronomy books that had been thrown out by people in his building.

"She would dream that she was on another planet," said Sister Eileen, who added that even though Denise is an extraordinary student, she "never comes across like she knows everything."

It cannot be easy. Denise's counselor, Mary P. Duggan, wrote last fall that her grade point average, 99.87, is the highest of "any student during the 30 years I have been in Cathedral."

Nearly all winners have applied to Ivy League colleges, where the scholarship money will be used to help with tuition, room and board. Denise's first choices are Columbia and Yale. Anahad O'Connor, who will be the first of seven brothers and sisters to go to college, wants to go to Harvard, Yale or Columbia. He says he plans to became a nuclear chemist.

But it is only with the award and other financial help that he can enroll anywhere. His mother, a teacher's aide, makes less than $18,000 a year. On the line in the scholarship application that asked whether his family had money in the bank, he wrote,

"$84.59."

QiQi Cheng's mother, who was persecuted during China's Cultural Revolution, is a waitress in a restaurant in Chinatown. She makes $7,000 a year, barely enough to pay their rent in Elmhurst.

In interviews with the students this week, all described lives of hardship and loneliness, made lonelier, they said, because they often had to turn away from friends and family to succeed academically.

"There is no middle ground for me," said Anahad, some of whose brothers and sisters did not finish high school. "Either I do well in school or I end up falling behind and stay in the neighborhood for the rest of my life."

80 In his application, he remembered being on the subway in junior high school and staring at students in well-pressed private-school uniforms.

The six scholarship recipients

85 "I envied them not simply because they were wealthy," he wrote, "but because they could afford the higher standard of education that I **coveted** so much." Later, when he could not

90 get an advanced chemistry course at his high school, he and his teachers managed to get him into the course at Stuyvesant, which is nearby.

Mirela Miraj spoke in her interviews for the scholarship of the suffering she experienced in Albania because she was a Catholic among a Muslim

95 majority. But once she got to New York, she **transformed** pain and bitterness into determination. "A man's soul is harder than a rock," she wrote in her application. "I have seen people who have suffered every **atrocity** and have still been able to survive and go on. Many of these people, including my parents, have inspired me along the way." She and her parents—her father is a

100 porter at Trump Tower—live with her older sister and her brother-in-law and their two young children in a small apartment in Ridgewood, Queens.

Elizabeth Murray, who bounced from apartment to apartment and often onto the park benches and streets of the Bedford Park section of the Bronx after her mother died, also found an unlikely **catalyst.** "I was poor, lived in a

105 rundown neighborhood and was neglected, left to raise myself," she wrote. "I found that I was an increasingly bitter person, resentful towards anyone who had the means I lacked." But she said that when she began living on the streets, not knowing where she would eat next, "something in me changed."

"I started to grasp the value of the lessons I was learning living on the

110 streets. I knew after overcoming these obstacles, next to nothing could hold me down."

She now supports herself, scraping by to pay rent in her own apartment with help from welfare. She has applied to Brown and Harvard.

At a welfare office recently, she recalled, she had to ask an interviewer to

115 hurry because she had an interview later with Harvard.

"The woman looked at me and rolled her eyes and said, 'Yeah, right, and that girl over there, she's got one at Yale.' "

Randy Kennedy

Copyright © 1999 by the New York Times, Co. Reprinted by permission.

GLOSSARY

adversity (n.) a state of hardship or affliction; misfortune

atrocity (n.) an extremely evil or cruel action, behavior, or condition

catalyst (n.) one situation that brings about another situation or event

commandeer (v.) to take arbitrarily or by force

covet (v.) to desire something that belongs to another person

feat (n.) a notable act or deed, especially an act of courage

harrrowing (adj.) extremely distressing; agonizing

persecute (v.) to oppress or harass with ill-treatment because of race, religion, or ethnicity

persevere (v.) to persist in a purpose, an idea, or a task in the face of obstacles or discouragement

statistical (adj.) having to do with the mathematics of collecting, organizing, and interpreting numerical data

stutter (n.) the act or habit of speaking with spasms in which word sounds are repeated or prolonged

transform (v.) to change the nature, function, or condition of something

valedictorian (n.) the student with the highest academic rank in a class who delivers the farewell address at graduation

virtually (adv.) practically; nearly; almost

QUICK COMPREHENSION CHECK ☑

Complete the sentences in this brief summary about the selection:

In this selection, Randy Kennedy tells about six students chosen from

(1) _____ to be the first recipients of

(2) _____.

Kennedy regards the group as a "statistical snapshot" of poor and working-

class students in the city; they represent diverse backgrounds, such as

(3) _____.

Yet, Kennedy stresses what these students have in common: **(4)** _____

_____.

To develop this point, he shares their personal stories. For example, while

escaping Yugoslavia on a military boat, Mirela experienced the horror of

(5) _____.

Another recipient, Elizabeth Murray, lost her mother to **(6)** _____.

After that, Elizabeth lived in **(7)** _____.

When being interviewed for this article, all the students described their lives as

(8) _____. They value education so much

that they often lose **(9)** _____.

QUESTIONS FOR THOUGHT AND DISCUSSION

1. What award did the six students receive?

2. Explain the selection's title.

3. Retell the story of one of the students featured in the selection.

4. Why does the author stress the significance of these students' achievements?

5. Describe the socioeconomic status of the students described in this selection. How do you know what their socioeconomic status is?

6. Explain what the author means when he says these students offer a snapshot of American society.

7. Tell about some of the hardships and obstacles the students overcame.

8. What is the main idea of this selection?

9. What message would this selection convey to immigrant students who want to go to college?

10. Do you know anyone whose dreams came true as these students' dreams did? Share what you know.

11. Explain how these students' lives may change in the future.

ANOTHER LOOK AT THE SELECTION

Supporting Details

The Quick Comprehension Check and the Questions for Thought and Discussion sections guided you to identify two important points the author wanted to convey to you, the reader:

   a. that the students receiving the scholarship were from diverse backgrounds

   b. that the students encountered obstacles in life that may have interfered with their goals for education

The author proved these points to you by providing adequate supporting details. You will identify some of these supporting details by completing the grid below. Do the following:

  1. Select three of the six students.

  2. For each student, enter these supporting details:

    a. name

    b. background information

    c. obstacles to education

STUDENT'S NAME	BACKGROUND INFORMATION	OBSTACLES TO EDUCATION
1.		
2.		
3.		

VOCABULARY BUILDING

Practice with Meaning and Context

> **VOCABULARY STRATEGY:** Vocabulary study is very important, but as you read, keep in mind that you are reading for the meaning of the selection. Do not get lost in the study of each word. Vocabulary exercises, like the ones in this text, will help you build your vocabulary so that reading for meaning will become easier in time. If you need to know the meaning of a word, the first thing to do is to try to get it from the context (the words and sentences around the word). If you cannot, you must look it up in a dictionary.

Practice determining meaning through context. A word or phrase is underlined in each of the following passages from or about the selection. Tell what the word or phrase seems to mean and explain how the surrounding language helped you determine this meaning.

1. Pulling off a 95 average in two years at the Humanities Preparatory Academy in Greenwich Village is almost unheard of.

Meaning or sense of the phrase _____

_____

Clues that suggest this meaning _____

_____

2. "The three students are among six who were chosen this week, from a pool of almost 3,000 applicants citywide."

Meaning or sense of the word _____

_____

Clues that suggest this meaning _____

_____

Other meanings for the word _____

_____

3. "Sister Eileen Regina, <u>moderator</u> of the marching band and a Spanish teacher at Cathedral High School at East 56th Street, said yesterday that Denise, 17, often told how she fell in love with science."

Meaning or sense of the word _____

_____

Clues that suggest this meaning _____

_____

_____

4. "But it is only with the award and other financial help that he can <u>enroll</u> anywhere."

Meaning or sense of the word _____

_____

Clues that suggest this meaning _____

_____

_____

IN YOUR WORDS

Your Path to College

Like the students described in the selection, you decided to go to college. Consider the path that led you to your college. Was this path filled with obstacles, or was it smooth and direct? Did you travel this path alone? Did others travel with you or guide you? Write your story on the following lines:

_____

_____

_____

_____

_____

_____

_____

_____

_____

_____

SUMMING UP

Share your thoughts in a group or with the class. What do others think?

1. How many classmates found similarities between their experiences and those of the students featured in the article? What were the specific similarities that your classmates cited?

2. Did everyone agree with the point that immigrants seeking an education in the United States are likely to face certain obstacles? If so, what particular obstacles did they cite? Did they find some obstacles to be more critical and challenging than others?

3. How have your classmates overcome the obstacles they encountered?

4. Why are you and your classmates in college?

5. What advice would you and your classmates give to young immigrants in the United States who want to go to college?

CLOSING THE CHAPTER

Role Play for Building Decision-Making Skills

With a partner or in a group, choose one or more of the following situations and brainstorm ways to resolve them. Your final project is to produce a skit that shows the process of making decisions. Use these questions to guide your work:

1. What decision do you need to make?

2. Whom will this decision affect?

3. What are the factors that you should consider?

4. What will you do?

5. Why?

6. How did you reach this decision?

7. How will you inform everyone involved?

8. What are the consequences of this decision?

Choose from these situations:

1. You receive both an acceptance letter from a college and an offer for full-time employment at the same time. You need to decide between the two. What will you do?

2. You are involved in a serious romantic relationship. Your parents, who still reside in your native country, have already arranged your marriage with a family in a neighboring village. How will you handle this situation?

3. You are involved in a serious romantic relationship much sooner in your life than you ever thought. You are a student; you do not think you are ready for marriage. The person you are involved with wants to get married soon. What will you do?

4. Your parent is ill and needs full-time care. Will you care for your parent in your home, or will you send your parent to a nursing home?

5. Your children attend a school where violent behavior is increasing. They are afraid to go to school, and their grades are dropping. You love your neighborhood, despite the problems at the local school, since your family and friends live there. How will you handle the problem your children are experiencing?

6. Your spouse, who lost his or her job recently, has been depressed and unmotivated about finding a new job. You have financial problems. Without the second income, you will not be able to pay your bills, especially your rent. What will you do to resolve this domestic problem?

7. Your child demonstrates athletic ability, and a teacher recommends sending him or her to a summer camp. The camp is quite expensive. Will you send your son or daughter or not?

REFLECTING AND SYNTHESIZING

1. Create a timeline showing life's major passages. Use this timeline as a basis for group discussion about the different decisions people must make during the course of their lives, the challenges they will confront, and the stages or passages they look forward to.

2. Freewrite on one or more of the following topics:

a decision you made

a joyful time in your life

a difficult period in your life

the stage of life you look forward to

the most important event in the human story of someone you know well

3

THE HEROES IN OUR LIVES

OPENING THOUGHT

Hero (n.) 1. In mythology and legend, a man, often of divine ancestry, who is endowed with great courage and strength, celebrated for bold exploits, and favored by the gods. **2.** A person noted for feats of courage or nobility of purpose, especially one who has risked or sacrificed his or her life. **3.** A person noted for special achievement in a particular field: *the heroes of medicine.* **4.** The principal male character in a novel, poem, or dramatic presentation.

The American Heritage College Dictionary

Think about the title, definition, and opening illustration that introduce this chapter. Answer the following questions:

1. What does the illustration tell you about people who are called heroes?

_____

_____

_____

_____

_____

2. Tell about the people in society or the people you know who would be eligible for the medal shown in the illustration. Why would they receive this medal?

_____

_____

_____

_____

_____

3. How does the dictionary definition of the word *hero* correspond with your ideas on the topic? Are the ideas the same or different? Explain.

_____

_____

_____

_____

_____

4. Write your working definition of the word *hero*. State in your words what it means to be a hero. Feel free to include examples in what you write.

_____

_____

_____

_____

_____

_____

_____

_____

_____

Share your thoughts with your partner, group, or class.

The selections in this chapter focus on heroes—personal heroes, private heroes, public heroes, and famous heroes. Read about how and why some people are heroes in the eyes of others. Formulate your working definition of the word *hero* and consider whether the people in the selections are, indeed, worthy of the title *hero*.

Selection 1

DISCOVER WHAT YOU THINK

1. What effect does a hero have on other people?

2. What are some of the things heroes do?

3. Explain what it means for someone to be a personal hero.

4. Who is your personal hero? Why?

5. Who are the people that consider you a hero in their lives?

6. Does a person have to be famous to be considered a hero?

PREVIEWING

Develop appropriate questions for previewing the selection. Refer to your course log; remember to consider the following features:

- the selection's title and author

- the photographs, if any, that accompany the piece

- words in bold print

- the format or layout of the piece

Ask yourself how the selection is related to the chapter's topic.

Read the first and last sections and restate what they tell you.

Write notes in your course log. List the questions you have. Tell what you expect to read about in the selection.

WIND BENEATH MY WINGS

It must have been cold there in my shadow,
to never have sunlight on your face.
You were **content** to let me shine,
that's your way,
5   you always walked a step behind.

So I was the one with all the glory,
while you were the one with all the strength.
A beautiful face without a name,
for so long,
10   a beautiful smile to hide the pain.

Did you ever know that you're my hero,
and everything I would like to be?
I can fly higher than an eagle,
'cause you are the wind beneath my wings.

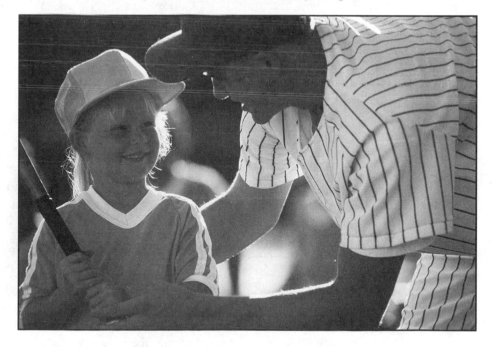

15
It might have appeared to go unnoticed,
but I've got it all here in my heart.
I want you to know I know the truth,
of course I know it,
I would be nothing without you.

20
Did you ever know that you're my hero,
and everything I would like to be?
I can fly higher than an eagle,
'cause you are the wind beneath my wings.

Fly, fly, fly away, you let me fly so high,
25
Oh fly, fly, so high against the sky,
so high I almost touch the sky,
Thank you, thank you, thank God for you,
the wind beneath my wings.

The Wind Beneath My Wings, by Larry Henley and Jeff Silbar. Copyright © 1982 Warner
House of Music & WB Gold Music Corp. All rights reserved. Used by permission.
WARNER BROS. PUBLICATIONS U.S. INC., Miami, FL. 33014.

GLOSSARY

content (adj.) satisfied

QUICK COMPREHENSION CHECK ✓

In Chapters 1 and 2 you completed the comprehension check by filling the
blanks in a summary paragraph for each selection. In this chapter, the quick
comprehension activity is different. You will no longer find summaries written
for you. Rather, you will be guided to develop your own skills for summarizing
information.

> **CONTROLLING IDEA:** To write an effective summary, you must
> understand and state the point or message of an entire section clearly in
> your own words. This point or message is called the **controlling idea** or
> **thesis.** It is the thought that unifies the piece. It is the thought to which all
> other content is connected. It is the central thought that all information,
> details, explanations, and analysis support.

1. What is the controlling idea of "Wind Beneath My Wings"?

    _____

    _____

    _____

2. What words or ideas in "Wind Beneath My Wings" express the controlling idea stated above? List at least three sections that make this controlling idea clear to you.

    a. _____

    b. _____

    c. _____

    d. _____

    e. _____

3. Using the information you provided for numbers 1 and 2 above, write a brief overview of what "Wind Beneath My Wings" is about.

    _____

    _____

    _____

    _____

    _____

QUESTIONS FOR THOUGHT AND DISCUSSION

1. "Wind Beneath My Wings" is a song. What is the purpose of this song?

2. Who is the person paying tribute to the hero?

    What do you know about the person?

    Can you guess his or her age, gender, and personal situation?

3. What did the hero do? Was it a specific action, a behavior, or an attitude?

    How do you know or how can you guess?

4. Describe the hero.

   Tell about his or her values and behaviors.

5. What effect does this hero have on others?

6. What people in everyday life does this hero represent? A parent? A teacher? A friend? A counselor? Tell what you think, and support your position with references to the song.

7. List some of the qualities heroes possess, as suggested in the song.

8. Tell whether the ideas in this song affect your views on who the heroes in our world are.

9. Who are the heroes in your life?

   What do they do?

   How are they similar to yet different from heroes described in the news or on television?

10. Are you someone's hero? Explain.

ANOTHER LOOK AT THE SELECTION

Repetition

In this selection, you read the lyrics—words—of the song "Wind Beneath My Wings." Like many songs, "Wind Beneath My Wings" repeats some of its lyrics. In this section, you will study the purpose for and effect of repetition.

1. Go back to the selection and identify a section that is repeated. Copy that section on the following lines:

   _____

   _____

   _____

   _____

   _____

   _____

2. What message does this section convey?

_____

_____

_____

_____

3. Why would the songwriter want to repeat this section, this message?

_____

_____

_____

4. What effect does the repetition have on you, the reader? Consider both the repetition of information, which might help with comprehension, and the repetition of sounds, which may bring pleasure or enjoyment.

_____

_____

_____

_____

5. How does repetition in music affect a listener?

_____

_____

_____

6. Are you familiar with religious or patriotic songs from the United States or your country that repeat lyrics? Tell what you know. Recite the words that are repeated, tell why they are repeated, and explain the effect they have on the people who sing or listen to the songs. Write your answers to this set of questions in your course log.

VOCABULARY BUILDING

Music Terms

Effective discussions about songs like "Wind Beneath My Wings" include words specific to the study of music. Some of these words are listed below, along with their definitions. You may want to record these music terms—and others that you or your classmates know—in your course log for future reference. It is not uncommon for college students to take introductory music courses. If that is your case, you will get a head start by reviewing the words here. Working with your classmates and using resources such as a dictionary, match the definitions and music terms.

Vocabulary

_____ **1.** lyrics

_____ **2.** composer

_____ **3.** score

_____ **4.** melody

_____ **5.** harmony

_____ **6.** lyricist

_____ **7.** refrain

Meanings

a. a writer of song lyrics

b. an arrangement of single notes that makes up a musical structure

c. a person who creates music

d. the words of a song

e. written music that shows instrumental and vocal parts

f. a phrase or verse repeated at intervals throughout a song

g. a combination of musical sounds considered to be pleasing

IN YOUR WORDS

Symbolism

The eagle, a symbol in the song "Wind Beneath My Wings," has symbolic meaning in other contexts. Think about the two levels of meaning the word *eagle* has.

1. What does an eagle in general represent? Think of qualities, behaviors, strengths, and values.

_____

_____

_____

2. In what ways are a hero and an eagle the same?

_____

_____

_____

_____

3. What aspects of American society and culture involve the image of an eagle? Consider as many possibilities as you can: bills and coins used in the United States; different logos, mottoes, or symbols for the government and country; or the songs, documents, or tributes (such as "The Pledge of Allegiance") to the country.

_____

_____

_____

_____

4. What does the eagle, as used in information about the United States, say about the image of this country?

_____

_____

_____

5. Do you agree with this image of the United States? Is the United States what you thought it would be before you immigrated here?

_____

_____

_____

_____

6. Do you have a symbol in your culture that is as strong as the symbol of the eagle is for the United States? Share this information with your class. Tell as much of the folklore and history about this symbol as you can.

_____

_____

_____

_____

_____

SUMMING UP

Share your thoughts in a group or with the class. What do others think?

1. Are any of your classmates familiar with the song "Wind Beneath My Wings"? How do they know about it? Did the information they shared improve the group's comprehension of the song's purpose and message?

2. How did your classmates react to the idea of a personal hero?

3. Who is the hero in the song? What possible interpretations did your classmates introduce?

4. Who are the heroes in your classmates' lives? What have these heroes done? How have your classmates expressed gratitude to their heroes?

5. Are your classmates heroes? What have they done?

6. Have your classmates' views on heroes changed at all after discussing this topic? Explain what has and has not changed.

Selection 2

DISCOVER WHAT YOU KNOW

1. What do movies, books, cartoons, or the news seem to say about what a hero is and what a hero does?

2. Explain how heroes in your daily lives are similar to or different from the heroes found in movies, books, cartoons, or the news.

3. Are the deeds heroes perform limited to physical feats—demonstrations of great strength? Explain your response.

4. What are some of the heroic deeds everyday people might perform?

PREVIEWING

Preview the selection, using your course log and what you have learned from other previewing sections. Write notes in your course log. List the questions you have. Tell what you expect to read about in the selection.

MAN STOPS TRUCK WITH HANDS
SAVES AILING CALIFON DRIVER'S LIFE

MENDHAM TOWNSHIP—A Hillsborough man jumped into a rolling lumber truck Wednesday and pushed the air brakes down with his hands as the driver lay **immobilized** by a **diabetic seizure.**

5   Scott Grote, 31, a machine operator at Public Service Electric and Gas Co., was driving south on Roxciticus Road at 9 A.M. when he stopped to allow a lumber truck to back into a new development, police said.

When five minutes passed and the lumber truck hadn't moved, Grote got out and found Robert Dugan, 47, of Califon, in the driver's seat, Patrolman John List said.

10   Grote ran to his truck and radioed his **dispatching** center for help. He then raced back to the lumber truck as it began to roll backward south on Roxciticus. He jumped into the truck and pushed down on the air brakes, holding it down with his hands.

He was unable to reach across to the parking brake, however, which was
15   on the passenger's side.

His foreman, Albert Garcia Jr., was only five minutes away as they were working on a new gas line at a development off Fox Chase Road. When he heard the call for help, he drove to the site, arriving just as Grote was holding down the brake.

20   Garcia put a wheel chuck behind the tires to keep the truck from rolling so that Grote could go around to the other side and activate the parking brake.

"It was an **adrenaline** rush. I didn't think about anything, I didn't have the time," Grote, of Hillsborough, said. "I don't feel like a hero, it was a 25   team effort and I was just in the right place at the right time."

Police, the first aid squad and the **mobile** intensive care unit arrived within minutes to find Dugan **conscious,** but **unresponsive.** Dugan's blood sugar level was dangerously low and he could have slipped into a **coma** and died, List said. They immediately started an **intravenous glucose** injection 30   and after 20 minutes Dugan was back to normal and released.

The PSE&G workers stayed to help direct cars, List said.

Authorities were not sure why the truck started rolling.

Laura Bruno
Reprinted with permission.

GLOSSARY

adrenaline (n.) a hormone that affects the blood vessels and blood pressure

coma (n.) a deep, prolonged unconsciousness, usually the result of injury, disease, or poison

conscious (adj.) having awareness of one's environment and self

diabetic (adj.) having to do with excess sugar in the blood

dispatch (v.) to send to a specific location

glucose (n.) a sugar that occurs widely in most plant and animal tissue and is the major energy source of the body

immobilize (v.) to stop movement

intravenous (adj.) within or administered in a vein

mobile (adj.) movable

seizure (n.) a sudden attack or spasm

unresponsive (adj.) not capable of reacting

QUICK COMPREHENSION CHECK ✔️

Writing a Summary

> **SUMMARY:** A **summary** is a short version of what you read. You retell what you read in your own words and in complete sentences. When you summarize, you must make sure you understand and remember the most important information in the reading selection. To write a good summary, you must be able to formulate a controlling idea, identify main ideas, and select important details and then restate this information in your own words. It is not appropriate to offer your opinion or to describe personal experiences in a summary.

Prepare to write a summary of "Man Stops Truck with Hands" by rereading the selection and doing the following:

1. Underline important details.

2. Write main ideas in the margin.

3. Write out the controlling idea for the entire piece.

Next review your marks and notes; make sure you have selected just enough detail to give an impression of the selection but not so much detail that you are virtually rewriting the piece.

Now begin to shape your notes for writing a summary. Work on your own or in a small group. Follow these steps:

a. Write out the controlling idea for the selection.

_____

_____

_____

b. List the main ideas and details that an effective summary should include.

_____

_____

_____

_____

_____

c. Shape the information you wrote above into an organized summary paragraph by combining ideas, eliminating repetition, making sure you include critical information, and checking the order in which you present information.

_____

_____

_____

_____

_____

_____

QUESTIONS FOR THOUGHT AND DISCUSSION

1. Why did Scott Grote get out of his car to check on Robert Dugan's lumber truck?

2. What problem did Scott find when he reached the lumber truck?

3. What did Scott do once he learned about this problem?

4. Based on the incident reported in this selection, how would you describe Scott Grote? What particular values and qualities does he seem to possess?

5. Many people would regard Scott as a hero for what he did. What did Scott have to say about the help he provided? Does he see himself as a hero?

6. What problem was the driver of the lumber truck experiencing?

7. What could have happened to the driver of the lumber truck if Scott had not assisted him?

8. Would most people react to the situation as Scott did? Why or why not?

9. How is Scott similar to yet different from the typical hero you might learn about in the news?

10. What adjectives would you use to describe Scott Grote?

ANOTHER LOOK AT THE SELECTION

Taking a Position

When asked about his quick thinking and effort to stop the rolling truck, Scott said,

> "It was an adrenaline rush, I didn't think about anything, I didn't have time. . . . I don't feel like a hero, it was a team effort and I was just in the right place at the right time."

Do you agree with Scott, or would you call him a hero? Does the author of the article regard him as a hero? Consider these important issues about the chapter's topic by answering the following questions:

1. How does the selection's title and subtitle suggest that Scott performed a heroic deed when he helped Robert Dugan?

_____

_____

_____

2. What specific heroic actions did Scott perform?

_____

_____

_____

_____

3. Why doesn't Scott see himself as a hero?

_____

_____

_____

_____

4. Does a person have to do something extraordinary—like save another person's life—in order to be considered a hero?

_____

_____

_____

_____

5. Do you believe Scott Grote is a hero? Support your position with references to your personal definition of a hero, with details from the selection, and with examples from your experiences and reading.

_____

_____

_____

_____

_____

VOCABULARY BUILDING

Human Qualities and Heroic Acts

Humans possess a number of qualities, such as patience, honesty, and loyalty. What other qualities do you know? Which of these qualities are heroes likely to possess? In this section increase your vocabulary, specifically the words you use to speak about human strengths and character. Brainstorm a general list of human qualities first. Then focus on the specific qualities heroes are likely to demonstrate.

1. Working independently or in a group, list the human qualities you know.

patience

honesty

loyalty

2. Now focus on and identify the specific human qualities heroes are likely to demonstrate. The following chart consists of two columns: one for heroic acts and one for human qualities. To complete the chart, list different heroic acts and then identify the human qualities that are needed to perform each heroic act. Information from the selection and other stories about heroes has already been entered into the chart.

HEROIC ACTS	HUMAN QUALITIES
1. saving a life	*courage, decisiveness*
2. jumping into a moving vehicle	*strength, courage*
3. entering a burning building	
4. descending into a collapsed mine	
5. shielding a human target	
6. donating an organ	
7.	
8.	
9.	
10.	
11.	
12.	

IN YOUR WORDS

Your Definition of a Hero

Express your thoughts.

1. Are certain people born to be heroes, or is it a particular situation or circumstance that forces people to be heroes whether they want to be or not?

   _____

   _____

   _____

   _____

2. Is the concept of a hero limited to performing extraordinary acts of physical strength, or can heroes be role models or people who perform acts of kindness?

   _____

   _____

   _____

   _____

3. Review what you wrote about the concept of a hero and summarize your personal thoughts on the topic.

   _____

   _____

   _____

   _____

   _____

SUMMING UP

Share your thoughts in a group or with the class. What do others think?

1. Do your classmates believe that Scott Grote is a hero? If all agree on this point, summarize the information they gave to support their views. If there is disagreement about this point, explain the nature of the disagreement and reasons for it.

2. What did your classmates say about Scott's statement about not being a hero? Do your classmates regard his statement as a sign of his strength or his weakness as an individual? Explain.

3. What definitions about a hero did your classmates share? Is there agreement among the group about who can be a hero, or is there disagreement? If your classmates agree on what makes a person a hero, summarize what they have to say. If members of the class disagree about what makes a person a hero, summarize the different views and explain the points in the definition that are controversial within the group.

4. What did your classmates say about the qualities heroes possess? What qualities does everyone in the group find essential for someone to be a hero?

Selection 3

DISCOVER WHAT YOU KNOW

1. What heroic deeds do you typically read about in the newspaper or see on television? Bring such an article to class. Is there a particular type of person or a particular profession that tends to be associated with these heroic deeds? Explain.

2. Can common people who are not necessarily trained to perform lifesaving acts be regarded as heroes? Explain.

3. How or why might a group of people have to work together to perform a heroic act? Can you tell about a group of people that worked together as heroes?

4. Consider the idea of a heroic act of generosity. What does this idea mean? Who might perform this type of act? Why? Tell about heroic acts of generosity you have learned about through the news, your reading, or your personal experiences.

PREVIEWING

Preview the selection, using your course log and the skills you practiced in other sections of this book. Record important points, observations, and questions in your course log.

HEROES FOR TODAY

LET THEM MAKE CAKE

After losing her job and home in 1984, Lynn Carr was living on the streets of St. Charles, Mo., with her five-year-old son. "We slept in our car for about a week," she said, "but it was **repossessed.**"

As she moved from one friend's house to another, Carr began working
5 toward a high-school **equivalency** diploma, listening to self-help tapes—and making cheesecakes. After developing some recipes she thought were pretty good, she offered her cakes to a restaurant. They sold out in a matter of hours.

The following year she met a man at a church service; they married after
10 a short **courtship.** Carr began selling cheesecakes out of their home, then later opened Twainland Cheesecake Company and Café in Hannibal. As business started booming, Carr didn't forget where she came from.

All of the women she hires are **welfare** moms or high-school dropouts—the workers most employers **shy away** from. As her dozen staffers create
15 100 to 150 cakes a week in the café's kitchen, **motivational** speakers on videotapes spread words of encouragement, stressing self-esteem and the work **ethic.**

Carr, who credits her employees for her success, says that as the company expands, "we're going to have a learning center and a daycare
20 center on site." Part of the workday will be spent studying for high-school-equivalency diplomas.

Recently a 33-year-old woman trying to raise three children on welfare was referred to Carr, who hired her on the spot. "It's been a real blessing," the woman said.

Jim Salter
Reprinted with permission of The Associated Press.

LIFESAVING TEAM

25   Karen Krynsky parked her blue Toyota at a Dexter, Fl., strip mall one day in February 1999. "I'll come open the door for you," she told her four-year-old grandson, Barry Lannen, in the back seat.

Before Krynsky could even close her door, the car **lurched** forward. "Nana, the car is rolling!" Barry **wailed.** Krynsky jumped into the driver's
30   seat and reached for the emergency brake, her left leg dragging outside, trying to stop the car. She couldn't find the brake, and she tumbled out of the car as it rolled down the steep slope toward a pond 20 feet away. A frightened Barry cried "Nana!" as the car splashed into the pond and water began pouring in.

35   "Help!" Krynsky screamed as the car **bobbed** away from shore. "My grandson's trapped inside!"

Gas station attendant, Mike Gleason, 21, had just stepped outside for a break when he saw a crowd by the pond. He sprinted down the slope and dived into the **numbingly** cold water.

40   Reaching the car, Gleason saw Barry's terrified face just inches above the water. "Unlock the door!" Gleason shouted. The boy's fingers **fumbled** with the childproof lock.

Gleason **pounded** on the rear window, but the glass wouldn't break. **Bystander** John O'Neill dived in and handed him a hammer. Grabbing it,
45   Gleason told the boy to move aside, and shattered the glass. He **groped** through the broken window in the black water and pulled the **gasping**

boy free. At that moment the last flash of blue metal disappeared beneath the water.

"Climb onto my back," Gleason said. Barry did so, but the exhausted man couldn't swim back. O'Neill, still beside them in the water, picked up Barry and swam to shore.

Later, doctors found Barry had suffered only mild **hypothermia.**

"They risked their lives to save Barry," Krynsky says of the men. "I thank God every day for them."

A PERSONAL PRESENT

Miki Hsu Leavey and Mary Groves barely knew each other. Every month for three years, Leavey, 44, would make deposits with teller Groves, 41, at a bank in Napa, Calif. They'd chat for a few minutes, but it was a casual friendship.

Then one day in May 1996, Leavey told Groves, "I need a kidney, and I just found out that no one in my family can give it to me." She said she'd be meeting with a transplant team at the University of California at San Francisco.

Leavey's kidneys had been severely scarred by lupus, a usually **chronic** disease that can **wreak havoc** with the immune system and organs throughout the body. Doctors said the wait for a kidney would be at least three years. "I thought about death and what it would mean for my husband and two children," Leavey said.

A month later, when Leavey met with the transplant team, one of the nurses said, "So tell me about your **donor.**"

"What donor?" Leavey asked.

"Mary," she said.

Leavey was **mystified.** Then she learned that Groves had tracked down the transplant team and volunteered to be the **donor.** "Oh, my God," said Leavey, **awestruck.**

When Leavey next saw Groves, she burst out crying and hugged her. "Any words seemed **superficial,**" Leavey said later. "What she did is **unfathomable.**"

Groves said giving her kidney was something she automatically knew was right. "It just came on me that I'll try," she said.

In December 1996 doctors put one of Grove's kidneys into Leavey. The surgery was successful, and both women are doing well.

"A Personal Present," by Jennifer Coverdale, *Napa Valley Register,* December 12, 1996. Reprinted by permission of the *Napa Valley Register.*

GLOSSARY

LET THEM MAKE CAKE

courtship (n.) the act or behavior of seeking attention for romantic reasons

equivalency (n.) equality

ethic (n.) a principle or value

motivational (adj.) able to move to action

repossess (v.) to regain possession

shy away (v.) to draw back, as from fear

welfare (n.) financial or other aid provided, especially by a government, to people in need

LIFESAVING TEAM

bob (v.) to move or cause to move up and down

bystander (n.) one who is present at an event without participating

fumble (v.) to mishandle or drop something

gasp (v.) draw or catch the breath sharply, as from shock

grope (v.) to search blindly or uncertainly

hypothermia (n.) abnormally low body temperature

lurch (v.) to roll or pitch suddenly

numbingly (adv.) in a way showing inability to move or feel normally

pound (v.) to strike repeatedly and forcefully

wail (v.) to cry loudly and mournfully, as in grief or protest

A PERSONAL PRESENT

awestruck (adj.) full of a mixture of wonder, dread, and reverence

chronic (adj.) of long duration; continuing or lingering

donor (n.) one who contributes, gives, or donates

havoc (n.) disorder or chaos

mystified (adj.) perplexed or bewildered

superficial (adj.) shallow; concerned with the surface only

unfathomable (adj.) unbelievable; incomprehensible

wreak (v.) to inflict

QUICK COMPREHENSION CHECK ✓

Choose one of the three stories in this selection and reread it carefully to
understand the controlling idea, main points, and most important details.
Use your own words to retell this information in a brief summary paragraph.

_____

_____

_____

_____

_____

_____

_____

Think about why you chose to write a summary for this story. Was it because you understood the material, liked the piece, or felt you could write an effective summary? Tell all the reasons that explain your choice.

_____

_____

_____

_____

_____

_____

_____

_____

QUESTIONS FOR THOUGHT AND DISCUSSION

1. How have these three brief stories about different heroes helped you, a reader who is studying the concept of a hero?

2. What was the heroic act that Lynn Carr performed? Why was she sensitive to the needs of a particular type of woman?

3. How did Lynn Carr become a hero? Did her success just happen, or did she work to achieve it? Explain.

4. What potential disaster did Karen Krynsky and her grandson face in February 1999?

5. Who assisted Karen at this time? What did these individuals do and what did they risk? How did the story end?

6. What problem did Mary Groves have? What role did Miki Hsu Leavey play in solving this problem?

7. What kind of person is Miki Hsu Leavey? How did Mary Groves react to what Leavey did?

8. Identify the heroes in this selection's three stories. Tell what they did. Do you see each as a hero? Do any stand out as being more of a hero than the others? Why? Do these heroes' actions match or conflict with your definition of a hero, as it is developing through your work in this chapter? Explain how.

ANOTHER LOOK AT THE SELECTION

More Practice with Summarizing

Choose another story from the selection and write a summary of its contents. Read the story carefully to understand its controlling idea, main points, and supporting details. Report this information in your own words and in complete sentences.

_____

_____

_____

_____

_____

_____

_____

_____

_____

_____

VOCABULARY BUILDING

Using Words in the Glossary

Seven of the words listed in the Glossary will fit in the seven blanks in the following sentences. Complete the sentences with the appropriate words, using the Glossary for assistance. When necessary, change the form of the words you use to fit the sentence.

TIP: The seven words selected for this exercise are strong action verbs that show sound or movement.

1. When Jose saw the truck careening toward him, he slammed on the brakes. His children _____ forward and bumped into the front seat.

2. Merlita was nervous as she prepared to leave her home forever. Her hands shook, and she _____ with the zipper on her bag.

3. The young mother could not sleep. Her baby was _____; she could not help but think that something was wrong with him.

4. Xiu _____ for the doorknob in the dark; he did not want to turn the lights on and risk having his parents learn that he had stayed out most of the night.

5. The police _____ on the door, hoping to wake the suspect.

6. Anna did not know how to swim. Her head _____ in the water for several moments, and then she went under.

7. When Sue saw the shadow in her room, she _____. Hearing her, the intruder jumped forward.

IN YOUR WORDS

Comparing and Contrasting Information

Do heroes perform courageous acts for different reasons? Explore how heroes can be similar to yet different from one another by examining the heroes in two of this selection's stories. Use the following t-bar to map out the similarities and differences you find. Then answer the questions to formulate general statements about how and why heroes are alike, different, or both.

Hero: _____   Story: _____

Hero: _____   Story: _____

SIMILARITIES	DIFFERENCES

1. Why did you choose to analyze these two heroes?

_____

_____

2. What heroic acts did these persons perform? Are these actions similar to one another or quite different from one another? Explain.

_____

_____

_____

_____

3. Why did these persons act in heroic ways? Are their reasons for performing heroic acts similar to one another or different?

_____

_____

_____

4. Overall, are the two heroes you studied similar to or different from one another? In your view, is one of them more of a hero than the other? Explain.

_____

_____

_____

_____

SUMMING UP

Share your thoughts in a group or with the class. What do others think?

1. What did you and your classmates say about writing summaries? Is it a skill that you have mastered or one that needs practice? How can you and your classmates use summarizing effectively in your work for other courses? Do you think you will ever use summarizing skills when taking a test? Explain.

2. What did you and your classmates find when you compared and contrasted two heroes from different stories in the selection? Did all the heroes have something in common, or were they different from one another? Tell what the common feature was, or list the differences that made each hero distinct from the others.

3. How are you and your classmates doing with your personal definitions of the word *hero?* Did your thoughts change at all after reading the three stories in this selection? What changes did you make? Why?

4. Do you and your classmates believe that all the people mentioned in the three stories are true heroes? Why or why not?

5. Why are some people heroes and others not? What would you and your classmates have done if you had been faced with the situations described in the three different stories?

Selection 4

DISCOVER WHAT YOU KNOW

1. How did the people of the world react to the death of Diana, Princess of Wales? Why was she so popular?

2. What do you know about Diana's family and childhood? Her marriage to Prince Charles? Her personal problems?

3. How did Diana react to the media? Why?

4. What causes did Diana champion? What were her reasons for supporting and fighting for these causes? What contemporary heroes did Diana spend time with? What did her contact with these individuals say about both her and them?

5. What did Diana try to teach her sons?

6. What legacy did Diana leave behind for the people of the world?

PREVIEWING

Preview the selection, using the skills you practiced in other sections of this book. Record important points, observations, and questions in your course log.

THE PRINCESS DIANA

Why could we not avert our eyes from her? Was it because she beckoned? Or was there something else we longed for?

This selection was included in *Time Magazine's* 1999 five-part series on the one hundred heroes of our time.

What was it about Diana, Princess of Wales, that brought such huge numbers of people from all walks of life literally to their knees after her death in 1997? What was her special appeal, not just to the British subjects but also to people the world over? A late spasm of royalism hardly explains it, even in Britain, for many true British monarchists **despised** her for cheapening the royal institution by behaving more like a movie star or a pop **diva** than a princess. To many others, however, that was precisely her attraction.

Diana was beautiful, in a fresh-faced, English, outdoors-girl kind of way. She used her big blue eyes to their fullest advantage, melting the hearts of

10 men and women through an expression of **vulnerability.** Diana's eyes, like those of Marilyn Monroe, contained an appeal directed not to any individual but to the world at large. Please don't hurt me, they

15 seemed to say. She often looked as if she were on the verge of tears, in the manner of folk images of the Virgin Mary. Yet she was one of the richest, most glamorous and socially powerful women in the world. This

20 combination of vulnerability and power was perhaps her greatest **asset.**

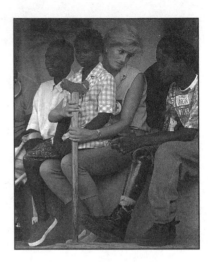

Diana's eyes, appealing to others

Diana was a princess, but there are many princesses in Europe, none of whom ever came close to capturing the popular

25 imagination the way she did. Princess Grace of Monaco was perhaps the nearest thing, but then she had really been a movie star, which surely provided the vital **luster** to her role as figurehead of a country that is little more than a gambling casino on the southern coast of France. The rather **louche** glamour

30 of Monaco's royal family is nothing compared with the fading but still **palpable** grandeur of the British monarchy. To those who **savor** such things, British royals are the first among equals of world royalty, the last symbols of an aristocratic society that has largely disappeared in most places but still hangs on, with much of its Victorian **pomp** intact, in Britain. Even the

35 Japanese Emperor Hirohito never forgot being overawed by the style of his British royal hosts on his first trip to Europe in the 1920s.

Diana not only married into British monarchy but was the offspring of a family, the Spencers, that is at least as old as the British royal family and considers itself in some ways to be grander. It is not rare in England to hear

40 the Spencers' Englishness compared favorably with the "foreign" (German) background of the Windsors. The famous speech, given by Diana's younger brother, the Earl of Spencer, at her funeral in London, with its barely contained **hostility** toward his royal in-laws, moved many people at the time but was in fact an exercise of extraordinary **hauteur.**

45 So Diana had **snob** appeal to burn. But that alone would not have secured her popularity. Most of the people who worshipped her, who read every **tidbit** about her in the gossip press and hung up pictures of her in their rooms, were not social snobs. Like Princess Grace of Monaco, Diana was a celebrity royal. She was a movie star who never actually appeared in a

50 movie; in a sense her whole life was a movie, a **serial melodrama** acted out

in public, with every twist and turn of the plot reported to a world audience. Diana was **astute** enough to understand the power of television and the **voracious** British tabloid newspapers. And she consistently tried to use the mass media as a stage for projecting her image—as the wronged spouse, as the radiant society beauty, as the compassionate princess hugging AIDS patients and land-mine victims, and as the mourning princess crying at celebrity funerals.

However, like many celebrities before her, she found out that she couldn't turn the media on and off at will, as though they were a tap. They needed her to feed the public appetite for celebrity gossip, and she needed them for her public performance, but what she hadn't bargained for was that her melodrama ran on without breaks. Everything she said or did was fair copy. After deliberately making her private life public, she soon discovered there was nothing private left. . . .

Wearing protective equipment, Diana tours a minefield during a visit to Angola.

Diana was a sacrificial symbol in several ways. First she became the patron saint of victims, the sick, the **discriminated** against, the homeless. Then, partly through her real suffering at the hands of a rigidly formal family trained to play rigidly formal public roles, and partly through her **shrewd manipulation** of the press, Diana herself projected a **compelling** image of victimhood. Women in unhappy marriages identified with her; so did outsiders of one kind or another, ethnic, sexual or social. Like many religious **idols,** she was openly abused and **ridiculed,** in her case by the same press that stoked the public worship of her. And finally she became the ultimate victim of her own fame: pursued by **paparazzi,** she became a twisted and battered body in a limousine. It was a fittingly **tawdry** end to what had become an increasingly tawdry melodrama. But it is in the nature of religion that forms change to fit the times. Diana—celebrity, tabloid princess, *mater dolorosa* of the pop and fashion scene—was, if nothing else, the perfect idol for our times.

Ian Buruma

Copyright © 1999 Time, Inc. Reprinted by permission.

GLOSSARY

asset (n.) a useful or valuable quality, person, or thing

astute (adj.) showing keen judgment

compelling (adj.) forceful

despise (v.) to dislike intensively

discriminate (v.) to make distinctions, often on the basis of prejudice

diva (n.) goddess

hauteur (n.) arrogance

hostility (n.) deep-seated, often mutual hatred

idol (n.) one who is adored

louche (adj.) not decent; not reputable

luster (n.) brilliance or radiance

manipulation (n.) tampering or falsification for personal gain

mater dolorosa **(n.)** mother of sadness

melodrama (n.) a drama marked by exaggerated emotions, stereotypical characters, and interpersonal conflicts

palpable (adj.) easily perceived; obvious

paparazzi (n.) photographers who stalk celebrities

pomp (n.) magnificent display; splendor

ridicule (n.) words or actions intended to evoke contemptuous laughter at a person or thing

savor (v.) to appreciate fully

serial (n.) a literary or dramatic work published or produced in installments

shrewd (adj.) marked by keen awareness and a sense of the practical

snob (n.) one who acts superior to or better than others

tawdry (adj.) shameful; indecent

tidbit (n.) a choice piece

voracious (adj.) exceedingly eager; hard to satisfy

vulnerability (n.) weakness

QUICK COMPREHENSION CHECK ✅

Reread the selection carefully to understand the controlling idea, main points, and most important details. Mark this information when you read, or take notes in your course log. Using your own words and writing in complete sentences, give the highlights of the selection in a brief summary paragraph.

_____

_____

_____

_____

_____

QUESTIONS FOR THOUGHT AND DISCUSSION

1. Why were people drawn to Diana?

   What was unique about her appearance?

   What did her eyes seem to say?

2. How was Diana different from the other princesses of Europe?

   How much did these differences have to do with the British monarchy?

   How did Diana herself create these differences?

3. How does the author portray the British monarchy?

   What is the author's attitude toward the British monarchy?

   How do you get a sense of this attitude?

4. What does the author say about Diana's family, the Spencers?

   What new information did you learn about Diana's background?

5. What does the author say about the speech Diana's brother gave at her funeral? What was the tone of the speech? How did the common people respond to it? How did the speech reveal information about the Spencers' social status?

6. What image did Diana wish to project?   What type of people would find this image appealing? What groups of people benefited from the image she projected?

7. How did the media and Diana need one another? How did Diana use the press? What happened when Diana opened her life to the media?

8. What did the author mean when he said that Diana was a sacrificial symbol?

   Why was Diana a victim? Who had victimized her?

   What other victims did Diana represent?

9. What is a religious idol?

   How do people tend to react to a religious idol?

   Why did the author compare Diana to religious idols?

10. Explain what the author meant when he wrote that Diana was a victim of her fame.

ANOTHER LOOK AT THE SELECTION

The Double-Entry Journal

DOUBLE-ENTRY JOURNAL: A double-entry journal is a specially formatted journal that is helpful for reading and understanding material that focuses on issues and controversy. The double-entry journal consists of two columns. In one you write the opinions and views an author states in a selection; in the other you write your response to or analysis of the author's views. This format shows your ideas next to those of the author; it will help you analyze information more easily and think or write about it in an organized manner.

The following diagram shows what a double-entry journal looks like and does:

TITLE OF SELECTION

AUTHOR'S IDEAS	MY IDEAS
Note facts, issues, examples, and opinions that you need to address in your decision about the topic or issue.	State your knowledge and thoughts about the topic as well as the questions, inferences, and opinions you have.

Now complete your double-entry journal for "The Princess Diana." Focus on the central issue the author explores: whether Diana is or is not a hero of our time.

THE PRINCESS DIANA

AUTHOR'S IDEAS	MY IDEAS

VOCABULARY BUILDING

Word Forms and Gender

In your discussions about Princess Diana, your vocabulary will be more precise if you use the form of the word *hero* that refers to a woman. Do you know this word? If not, can you find it in the dictionary? If not, does a classmate know the word? Check all resources possible; write the form of *hero* that refers to a

woman: _____

A. There are many examples of word pairs in English that are differentiated by gender. That is, two words for a particular type of person exist; one refers to males and the others to females. Can you think of other examples?

Write the pairs you know here:

B. The word pairs that distinguish gender may differ slightly in form or be completely different from one another. You will practice this concept by filling in the chart that follows. In the left column are 12 words for a male who performs certain acts or has a certain identity. In the right column, write the corresponding word for a woman. Work with your classmates to complete the pairs and to add two new pairs. The first two are done for you.

MALE	FEMALE
1. father	*mother*
2. brother	*sister*
3. uncle	
4. nephew	
5. king	
6. prince	
7. groom	
8. widower	
9. actor	
10. waiter	
11. hero	
12. host	
13.	
14.	

IN YOUR WORDS

The selection about Diana is one of a five-part series on the 100 heroes and icons of our time according to *Time Magazine*. The author introduces issues about Diana, hoping to get you, the reader, to determine whether she is indeed a heroine. Three words are critical to this series about heroes and the selection about Diana. These three words are *hero, icon,* and *idol.*

Work with your classmates to define these three words and distinguish them from one another.

1. Start by defining the three terms. Aim for working definitions that show your understanding of the terms rather than word-for-word dictionary definitions. Provide examples for each working definition. You may use the heroes featured in the chapter's selections if you wish.

hero

Working definition _____

_____

_____

_____

Examples _____

_____

idol

Working definition _____

_____

_____

_____

Examples _____

_____

icon

Working definition _____

_____

_____

_____

Examples _____

_____

2. What are the basic differences among the three words?

_____

_____

_____

_____

_____

3. Can someone be a hero, idol, and icon? Explain. If so, give an example.

_____

_____

_____

_____

SUMMING UP

Share your thoughts in a group or with the class. What do others think?

1. Do your classmates accept the idea that Diana deliberately used the media to project herself as a victim? Was she really a victim? If so, a victim of what?

2. Did your classmates feel that Diana should indeed be listed among *Time Magazine*'s 100 heroes and icons of our time? If your classmates were in agreement, summarize their position. If your classmates disagreed, summarize the points of disagreement.

3. What conclusions did your classmates come to about the differences between the words *hero, idol,* and *icon?* Which of the words would they use to describe Diana?

4. In the days following her death, stories about Diana were often accompanied by photographs of her with other heroes of our time—Mother Teresa and the Pope, for example. Would you and your classmates classify Diana with such extraordinary people? Why or why not?

5. Is Diana, Princess of Wales, a hero of our time? What did your classmates say about this? What are arguments supporting this status for Diana? What are arguments against this status for Diana?

CLOSING THE CHAPTER

Synthesize what you know. Think about the selections, what you hear on the news or read in the paper about heroes, and your personal experiences with or knowledge about heroes. Use this information to shape your personal definition of the word. Include the qualities you think heroes possess and examples of people who, in your eyes, are the heroes of our times.

REFLECTING AND SYTHESIZING

Group Work: A Collage

Search for photographs that show heroic efforts and events. Discuss your work as you go along to sharpen your understanding of how you and your classmates define the concept of a hero. Mount your photographs on a poster board, provide captions for some of the photos, and develop a title for the collage that conveys its message about heroes.

Individual Work: Freewriting

Freewrite on one or more of the following topics:

a day when you were a hero

why you wish you were a hero

heroic qualities

your personal hero

a heroic event you witnessed

heroic professions

a hero in a movie

a hero on television

a hero in literature

how the media create heroes

4

COPING WITH TRAGEDY
AND DESTRUCTION

OPENING THOUGHT

These are the times that try men's souls.

Thomas Paine

The American Crisis, No. 1 (1776)

Think about the chapter's title, quotation, and opening photograph and then answer the following questions:

1. Describe what you see in the photograph.

_____

_____

_____

_____

2. What have the people who live in this area experienced? How will they rebuild their lives?

_____

_____

_____

_____

3. How could the situation shown in this photograph "try a person's soul"? What is the unique meaning of the word *try* in the quotation?

_____

_____

_____

_____

4. Tell what you know about the chapter's topic, using personal experiences, what you know about other people, and information from your studies and reading.

_____

_____

_____

_____

This chapter focuses on events that have brought tragedy and destruction to people in different parts of the world. Learn about these events and explore how human beings respond to and cope with disaster. As you read the selections and complete the exercises, write your thoughts about the chapter's content in your course log.

Selection 1

DISCOVER WHAT YOU KNOW

1. What is a hurricane? Describe the weather conditions that are typical during a hurricane and tell how they affect both people and the environment.

2. What areas of the world are most affected by hurricanes? Why?

3. What other natural phenomena can bring about the destruction that a hurricane does?

4. Share your personal experiences with or knowledge about a natural disaster like a hurricane. Include specific details. Tell where and when the natural disaster occurred, whom it affected, and how those affected by it coped during and after the event.

PREVIEWING

Preview the selection, using notes from your course log and what you have learned from other previewing sections. Write notes in your course log. List the questions you have. Tell what you expect to read about in the selection.

MURDEROUS MITCH

The hurricane that *devastated* Central America killed thousands and *slaughtered* the hopes of millions

Tragedy is numbingly routine in Central America. Poverty, earthquakes and civil wars have **savaged** the region for most of this century. Still, the Dantesque [like the poet Dante's descriptions of destruction and misery] **calamity** that hit the **isthmus** last week may have taken suffering to a new
5 **plateau.** As many as 10,000 people were estimated dead in the battered countries of Nicaragua and Honduras, while some 2 million were left homeless, in the wake of the **relentless** rains of Hurricane Mitch. In all, the storm caused a **staggering** $3 billion in damage—more than half the combined Nicaraguan and Honduran **gross domestic products.**
10 In Nicaragua alone, where 3,800 were thought dead, much of the landscape looks as **barren** as the moon. Starving, **sallow**-skinned children, many suffering **cholera** from the **fetid** waters that destroyed their homes, begged for food on the crumbled, mud-slick roads between Managua and the flooded northern **sierras.**
15 For towns like the once **thriving** community of Posoltega, nestled on rich soil beneath the Casitas Volcano in Nicaragua's mountainous northwest, Mitch was the **apocalypse.** Close to noon on Oct. 30, after the hurricane had dumped three days of rain into Casitas's crater, the mountainside burst with what villagers described as the angry roar of a jetliner. It **hurled** mud, water
20 and rock onto Posoltega's rooftops, "a terrible, towering wall that just fell out of the clouds," says Santo Díaz, 24. Díaz gathered his elderly father, mother, sister and two brothers to escape—but the avalanche claimed them. He was still clutching their hands as they were buried alive.
In Honduras, Mitch **spawned** the worst floods in 200 years. The waters
25 may have killed more than 5,000 people and left 11,000 missing. As Vice President William Handel helicoptered over the **deluged** Ulúa River valley, he saw three people trapped on a patch of high ground, waving **frantically.** The waters rose so fast that the **chopper** couldn't land—and Handel, just yards away, watched them drown, tossed like rag dolls in the **current.**
30 As the **gravity** of the disaster reached around the world, close to $100 million in aid poured in. But Central America's development, which

Mitch's destruction in Tegucigalpa, the capital of Honduras

lagged far behind the rest of the world before the hurricane, has been set
back decades.

Many if not most of Mitch's victims were youngsters—including not
35 only those who drowned but also those whose malnourished bodies were no
match for the deadly **septic** infections set free in the waters. Says Charles
Compton, local head of Plan International relief organization: "We have to
keep starvation and infection from claiming as many victims as the hurricane
did." When the final **tally** is in, the assertions of a **staggering toll** may well
40 be borne out. Those whom the floodwaters did not kill face the problems of
isolation, starvation, disease and neglect—the normal stuff of tragedy in
Central America made hundreds of times worse by Mitch's murderous rains.

Tim Padgett

Copyright © 1998 Time Inc. Reprinted by permission.

GLOSSARY

apocalypse (n.) great devastation; doom

barren (adj.) completely lacking

calamity (n.) a disaster

cholera (n.) an infectious, often fatal disease

chopper (n.) helicopter

current (n.) the flow of the water

deluged (adj.) flooded

devastate (v.) to destroy

fetid (adj.) having an offensive odor

frantically (adv.) acting in a crazed, anxious manner often due to anger or fear

gravity (n.) seriousness

gross domestic product (n.) the market value of a country's goods and services

hurl (v.) to throw forcefully; fling

isthmus (n.) a narrow strip of land connecting two larger masses of land

lag (v.) to fail to keep up in pace; straggle

plateau (n.) a stable level, period, or state

relentless (adj.) steady and persistent

sallow (adj.) of a sickly yellowish color

savage (v.) to assault ferociously

septic (adj.) causing toxins in the blood or tissue

sierra (n.) a rough, rugged range of mountains

slaughter (v.) to kill brutally or in large numbers

spawn (v.) to give rise to

staggering (adj.) overwhelming

tally (n.) the score or count

thriving (adj.) making steady progress

toll (n.) the amount or extent of loss and destruction, as in a disaster

QUICK COMPREHENSION CHECK ☑

Reread the selection carefully to understand the controlling idea, main points, and most important details. Mark this information when you read, or take notes in your course log. Using your own words and writing in complete sentences, give the highlights of the selection in a brief summary paragraph.

_____

_____

_____

_____

_____

_____

_____

_____

_____

_____

_____

QUESTIONS FOR THOUGHT AND DISCUSSION

1. Where did "Murderous Mitch" occur? What specific countries were affected?

2. List specific details that illustrate the destruction Mitch brought to the area.

3. Why was Mitch's effect on Posoltega particularly devastating? Consider the town's history, the way Mitch struck the town, and one survivor's personal tragedy.

4. What flooding conditions did Vice President William Handel of Honduras witness?

5. What particular segment of the population was most affected by Mitch? How? Why?

6. What effect did Mitch have on economic conditions in the countries it struck? Consider the estimated amount of damage as well as the general economic status and history of the area.

7. If Hurricane Mitch is seen as another event in the "numbing routine" of tragedy in Central America, then people of the region have coped with disaster before. What is it about human nature that makes coping possible?

   What qualities do people who cope with tragedy possess?

   What things do people do when they try to cope with tragedy?

8. What problems did Mitch's survivors have to cope with and overcome?

ANOTHER LOOK AT THE SELECTION

Understanding the Scope of the Tragedy

Trace the path of Hurricane Mitch on the map. To do this, return to the selection, find the names of the towns, rivers, and countries affected by Mitch. Then mark these locations on the map. Use a special code to mark areas that were hit particularly hard. After plotting Mitch's path on the map, answer the following questions:

1. How many miles of land and communities did Mitch destroy? Give an approximate total mileage from east to west. Give an approximate total mileage from north to south. Use the legend on your map to calculate these approximate distances:

   a. miles of destruction from east to west _____

   b. miles of destruction from north to south _____

2. What country had more communities destroyed than any other?

   _____

3. What countries or parts of countries remained relatively untouched by the hurricane?

   _____

   Why? _____

4. Examine the land formation of Central America. Why are hurricanes common in the area?

   _____

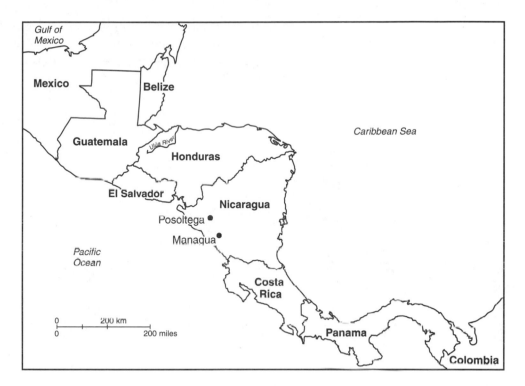

Gulf of Mexico

Mexico

Belize

Guatemala

Ulua River

Honduras

Caribbean Sea

El Salvador

Nicaragua

Posoltega •

Managua •

Pacific Ocean

Costa Rica

0   200 km

0   200 miles

Panama

Colombia

A regional map of Central America

LOOKING BEYOND THE SELECTION

Comparing Mitch with Other Hurricanes

To do this exercise, you must examine what you know about other hurricanes and search for additional information on the topic in the library or on the Internet. Use the information you gather to create a table of information about Hurricane Mitch and to draw conclusions about Mitch and how it compared to other hurricanes.

1. What do you know about other hurricanes that have taken place in Central America and other parts of the world? Refer to a specific hurricane by name or by the approximate date when it occurred. Tell what you know to your peers or write it in your course log.

2. Expand your knowledge. On your own or with your classmates, find information about at least three other hurricanes. Read this information, reread the selection, and complete the table below. Research the topic until you have filled every block in the table.

HURRICANE	WHERE	WHEN	EXTENT OF DAMAGE	CURRENT STATUS
Mitch				

3. Now refer to the table and answer these questions:

   a. Which hurricane occurred most recently? _____

   b. Where did the hurricane take place? _____

   c. What type of damage did this hurricane cause ? _____

   _____

   d. Which hurricane caused the most damage in terms of cost?

   _____

   e. Which hurricane destroyed more land than the others?

   _____

   f. Have any hurricane areas been completely rebuilt? Which ones?

   _____

VOCABULARY BUILDING

Build your vocabulary with knowledge about the types of different natural disasters that can occur. Using what you know, what your classmates know, and tools like a dictionary, match the following natural disasters with their definitions:

Natural Disasters

Definitions

_____ **1.** typhoon

_____ **2.** landslide

_____ **3.** earthquake

_____ **4.** tornado

_____ **5.** tidal wave

_____ **6.** flood

_____ **7.** drought

_____ **8.** hurricane

_____ **9.** volcanic eruption

a. a tropical storm involving heavy rains and winds exceeding 74 miles per hour

b. an overflowing of water onto normally dry land

c. an unusual rise of water along the seashore

d. a tropical storm in the West Pacific or Indian Ocean

e. a sudden movement of the earth's crust caused by stress from land faults or by volcanic activity

f. the ejection of lava, ashes, and gas through an opening in the earth's surface

g. a rotating column of air usually accompanied by a funnel-shaped downward cloud that moves destructively along a narrow path

h. a long period of low rainfall

i. the downward sliding of a mass of earth and rock

IN YOUR WORDS

Writing Generalizations

What generalizations about hurricanes can you make based on the information in your table?

> **GENERALIZATION:** A **generalization** is a statement that expresses an inference, a conclusion, an observation, or a principle. A generalization is based on evidence, and it has a broad application or meaning. The following sentences are generalizations: *Babies need a lot of sleep; knee injuries are common among soccer players; college is different from high school.*

Write your generalizations about hurricanes here:

1. _____

_____

_____

2. _____

_____

_____

3. _____

_____

_____

SUMMING UP

Share your thoughts about the selection in a group or with the class. What do others think?

1. What natural disasters have you and your classmates read about or experienced? What were the aftereffects of these occurrences? How did people cope with the disasters?

2. What natural disaster do you and your classmates regard as the worst of all possible disasters? Can you as a group decide on one natural disaster as being worse than all others? Why or why not? What are the points of disagreement if opinions differ?

3. What did you and your classmates learn about other hurricanes? How many hurricanes did your group or class learn about? In the opinion of the group or class, what is the worst hurricane of all time? Can you and your classmates decide on one hurricane? Why or why not?

4. What conditions must people who experience a hurricane deal with? How do they manage? What enables them to cope?

Selection 2

DISCOVER WHAT YOU KNOW

1. Tell what you know about space travel. Have you ever watched a spacecraft take off?

2. What significant events have occurred in the history of space travel? What are the major accomplishments of efforts to explore space?

3. Why do different countries sponsor space travel? What countries have strong space exploration programs?

4. Who can travel to space? What might someone do while in space? How does one train for space travel?

5. Have you ever seen photographs of or from space? Have you seen moon rocks or meteor rocks? Where have you seen these items?

PREVIEWING

Preview the selection, using your course log and what you have learned from other previewing sections. Write notes in your course log. List the questions you have. Tell what you expect to read about in the selection.

"CHALLENGER" EXPLODES—SHUTTLE FALLS INTO OCEAN; CREW APPARENTLY KILLED

The "Challenger" crew walking to the launch pad.

"We will never forget them (the astronauts), nor the last time we saw them, this morning, as they prepared for the journey and waved good-bye and 'slipped the surly bonds of earth' . . . ."

Ronald Reagan
January 21, 1986

The space shuttle *Challenger* exploded in a huge ball of red and yellow flame today and fell in blazing pieces into the Atlantic Ocean, apparently killing the seven astronauts aboard, including schoolteacher Christa McAuliffe.

5   The explosion of the $1.2 billion shuttle came at one minute, 15 seconds after launch when the shuttle was about 11 miles high and 9 miles down range from Kennedy Space Center. Out of the flame of the descending shuttle came objects still **belching** white smoke. They were apparently the

solid fuel **boosters** still firing. Huge chunks of the shuttle could be seen
10 falling into the water followed by the **billowing** smoke.

NASA made no announcement concerning the **fate** of the seven crew
members, including McAuliffe, the 37-year-old schoolteacher from New
Hampshire, the first **civilian** to be selected for a shuttle crew. Observers said
it was unlikely that anyone aboard survived.

15 There have been no **fatalities** in 55 previous manned U.S. space
missions. Today's explosion, however, occurred 19 years and one day after
three astronauts were killed on Jan. 27, 1967, in an explosion on the launch
pad in the Apollo space program.

Challenger exploded before the horrified eyes of spectators at the Florida
20 space center. The space shuttle, **plagued** by delays which included a
difficulty with ice forming on the structure that supported the shuttle, was
launched at 10:38 a.m. Houston time. It lifted off into a cloudless blue sky.
Trailing the usual thick white smoke, the main engines seemed to ignite

The shuttle "Challenger" exploding during lift-off.

properly. Everything seemed to be normal when with stunning suddenness
25 the shuttle exploded about 10:39:15 a.m.

Seconds before the crash, ground control radioed to spacecraft Cmdr.
Francis R. Scobee: "You're go for **throttle** up."

Scobee replied: "**Roger,** go at throttle up."

The explosion followed within seconds. Slow-motion TV monitors
30 showed what appeared to be a small explosion, possibly on the right solid
fuel rocket booster, followed by a massive eruption. The main external fuel
tank for the ship's three engines carried about 1.5 million pounds of liquid
hydrogen and oxygen.

The ship began to break up and fell blazing into the sea. Steve Nesbit, of
35 the public affairs office at Johnson Space Center, said: "Flight controllers are
looking very carefully at the situation. Obviously we have had a major
malfunction.

"We have no downlink," he said, meaning no radio signals were coming
from the shuttle.

40 Television monitors at the spaceport showed paramedics parachuting into
the sea near the shuttle's main impact point. A rescue force was **dispatched**
to try to track down the big pieces and see what might be done. NASA said
the main impact area appeared to be about 18 miles down course, but **debris**
rained down for miles. . . .

45 The explosion was a devastating tragedy for the National Aeronautics
and Space Administration after successfully carrying out 24 space shuttle
missions in slightly less than five years.

In addition to McAuliffe and Scobee, others on the crew were pilot
Michael Smith, mission specialists Judith Resnick, Ellison S. Onizuka and
50 Ron McNair and payload specialist Gregory Jarvis, an engineer with Hughes
Aircraft Co.

McAuliffe's husband, Steven, and her two small children, Scott and
Caroline, were among the spectators on hand to view the launch of the
4.5 million-pound, space freighter, the symbol of American technology.
55 McAuliffe's parents, Edward and Grace Corrigan, watching from the VIP
site 3½ miles from the launch pad, hugged each other and sobbed, watching
the fireball overhead. McAuliffe was to have taught two 15-minute lessons
on the fourth day of the mission. Public Broadcasting Service was to carry
the telecast live, and hundreds of schools planned to tune in. . . .

60 All 1,200 students at McAuliffe's Concord, N.H., High School were
cheering the televised launch when a teacher yelled for them to be silent
because something appeared to be wrong. As it became clear there was an
explosion, stunned students **murmured,** "This can't be real. . . . We can't be
watching this." Students, who were gathered in the auditorium, were ordered

65 back to their rooms. Many of the youths went **reluctantly,** protesting that they wanted to be allowed to continue watching.

Mary Ward, principal of Westwood Elementary School in Friendswood near Johnson Space Center where one of the NASA teacher-finalists Peggy Lathlaen teaches, said Lathlaen was in Florida and watched the launch and **70** crash with her husband Dave and her close friend. . . .

Ward was among those who supported Lathlaen's effort to be the first teacher in space. She said despite the tragedy Tuesday, she still believes the program should be pursued. "I think the civilian in space program will probably be approached more cautiously but I'm sure teachers and educators **75** would still like to be the first **civilians** in space. . . ."

President Reagan was watching when the craft exploded and "stood there in almost stone silence," White House spokesman Larry Speakes said. . . .

"It's a terrible thing," Reagan told reporters. "I just can't get out of my mind her (the teacher's) husband, her children, as well as the families of the **80** others on board."

In an account provided by an Independent News Network correspondent who attended a lunch at which Reagan spoke, the president expressed confidence in those running the space program and said those aboard were aware of the risks they were taking.

85 Asked what he would tell the nation's schoolchildren, who watched this flight more closely than others because a teacher was aboard and many special projects were planned for them, Reagan said: "You have to be out there on the frontier taking risks. Make it plain to them that life must go on. . . ."

90 It was the 25th shuttle flight and 10th for *Challenger.* The disaster was the worst for NASA since the first Apollo moon capsule burned on its launch pad Jan. 27, 1967, killing three astronauts. Of the four shuttles in NASA's stable—*Columbia, Challenger, Discovery* and *Atlantis*—*Challenger* had gained a reputation as a workhorse through its nine previous flights. But its **95** July mission got off to a frightening start. A launch try on July 12 ended in failure when its three main engines shut down seconds before liftoff. . . .

Icicles were the most recent problem to cause delay of launch. Space agency officials said subfreezing temperatures at Kennedy Space Center in Florida had produced icicles on the structure that supports the shuttle. The **100** early launch time was postponed about an hour because of the icicles.

Earlier, the space agency was forced to reschedule the launch of the shuttle *Challenger* from Monday to today because of mechanical and weather problems.

Carlos Byars

GLOSSARY

belch (v.) to gush forth violently

billowing (adj.) rolling or surging in waves

booster (n.) a rocket that provides the main thrust for the launch of a missile or space vehicle

civilian (n.) a person in the ordinary community; one not in the military or other special force

debris (n.) the scattered remains of something broken or destroyed; wreckage, rubble

dispatch (v.) to send to a specific location

fatality (n.) a death resulting from an accident or disaster

fate (n.) a final result; outcome

malfunction (n.) the failure to operate properly or normally

murmur (v.) to grumble and complain

NASA National Aeronautics and Space Administration

plague (v.) to bother

reluctantly (adv.) unwillingly; with hesitation

Roger (interj.) used in radio communications to indicate that a message was received

throttle (n.) a valve that regulates the flow of fluid, such as fuel

QUICK COMPREHENSION CHECK ✓

Reread the selection carefully to understand the controlling idea, main points, and most important details. Mark this information when you read, or take notes in your course log. Using your own words and writing in complete sentences, give the highlights of the selection in a brief summary paragraph.

_____

_____

_____

_____

_____

_____

_____

_____

_____

_____

_____

QUESTIONS FOR THOUGHT AND DISCUSSION

1. How long was the shuttle airborne before its malfunction was evident? Who were the *Challenger*'s crew members? What was unique about this particular group of people?

2. What did the shuttle explosion look like? What could people see from a distance? What did the slow-motion TV monitors show?

3. Who were the family members who watched in horror?

   What special communities witnessed this horrific event on TV? Why was this group of people watching the shuttle takeoff? How were they connected to the crew?

4. How did President Reagan, then President of the United States, react to the tragedy?

   What was his private response?

   What was his public message to the citizens of the country?

5. Until January 1986, what was *Challenger*'s reputation in the space program?

6. What are the different emotions that someone watching the launch would experience? Consider the emotions one would start with, the emotions associated with the thrill of witnessing a historic event; then consider the reality of the situation, the emotions of watching the unexpected take place.

7. Since *Challenger*'s launch was televised live, the horror of its explosion became a public event. How do you imagine people coped with the images they saw?

What other national and international events have been televised, bringing tragedy into the homes of the public? How do people cope with the tragedies they witness on TV?

ANOTHER LOOK AT THE SELECTION

Many people watched the shuttle explosion in horror. Among those people were individuals in roles of responsibility—most notably Steven McAuliffe, husband of Christie McAuliffe and father of their children, and scores of teachers throughout the United States, who watched the event with their students. At this difficult time, these individuals had to care for others. Analyze the difficult work of these individuals by exploring what they needed to do to protect as well as inform the people for whom they cared.

1. Who watched the shuttle launch with Steven McAuliffe? Were these individuals likely to understand the horror of the event they witnessed?

_____

_____

2. What was the age range of the different students throughout the United States who watched the shuttle launch that day? _____

3. What decisions did classroom teachers and Steven McAuliffe have to make that day—to protect, yet inform others?

_____

_____

4. In what ways were Steven McAuliffe's experience and the experiences of the classroom teachers similar? How did they differ? Why?

_____

_____

5. What human qualities are needed to cope with a tragedy of this type?

_____

_____

LOOKING BEYOND THE SELECTION

Weighing the Risks and Benefits of Space Travel

Why do countries like the United States invest a great deal of money in space travel? What is the purpose for traveling through outer space? What were some of the missions of the United States' different excursions to points in outer space? Gather information about space travel, and in light of the *Challenger* explosion, formulate your opinion about the risks or benefits of space travel. Look beyond the selection and answer these questions:

1. Using reference materials, electronic searches, and knowledge you and your classmates already possess, gather information about the missions of five different shuttle flights, including that of the *Challenger*. List what you find in the following table:

SHUTTLE FLIGHT/DATE	MISSION/PURPOSE	MISSION SUCCESSFUL? WRITE *YES* OR *NO*.
Challenger January 28, 1986	1. to start the civilian-in-space space program 2. to broadcast lessons from space	No

2. Is space travel more successful than unsuccessful? Or more unsuccessful than successful? Support your answer.

_____

_____

3. What are some of the reasons for traveling in space? Do these reasons outweigh possible risks? Explain your response.

_____

_____

_____

4. State your opinion about space travel.

_____

_____

5. Did you search for information about shuttle flights on the Internet? If so, what was the quality of the information you found? Was it worse than, similar to, or better than what you found through more traditional research methods?

_____

_____

_____

VOCABULARY BUILDING

Write your own sentences. Use words from the Glossary to replace the underlined words in the directions for each sentence.

1. Write a sentence about police investigators who were <u>sent directly to the scene</u> of a bank robbery.

_____

_____

2. Write a sentence about <u>people in the ordinary community</u> who were arrested for refusing to obey the police.

_____

_____

3. Write a sentence about students who returned to school <u>unwillingly</u> after summer vacation.

_____

_____

4. Write a statement about what the <u>outcome</u> will be for someone who immigrates to the United States.

_____

_____

5. Write a sentence about a car accident and the number of people injured and the number of <u>people killed</u>.

_____

_____

IN YOUR WORDS

Lines 87–89 contain a direct quote from President Ronald Reagan, who, when asked what to say to American's schoolchildren about the *Challenger* explosion, replied, "Make it plain to them that life must go on." Examine the President's advice and answer the following questions:

1. What did the President mean by his comment? State its central point in your own words:

_____

_____

_____

2. Why was the President's message particularly meaningful for young people?

_____

_____

3. What were some of the things that the citizens of the United States probably did to follow the President's advice?

_____

_____

_____

4. When during the course of our lives, with its pathways and passages, are we likely to have someone remind us that "life goes on"?

_____

_____

_____

5. Have you ever advised someone that "life goes on"? Whom did you advise? When? Why? How did the person respond to what you said?

_____

_____

_____

SUMMING UP

Share your thoughts about the selection in a group or with the class. What do others think?

1. One could say that *Challenger*'s explosion was a tragedy on many levels; that is, it was a sorrowful moment for different people for different reasons. Identify the groups affected by the event; tell what the impact was and how this impact was similar yet different for the various groups affected.

2. What realities about life did people face the day *Challenger* exploded? What things did they say to comfort themselves and others? What did they do to comfort themselves and others? What other life events require the same coping mechanisms that the *Challenger* explosion did?

3. What was unique about this particular shuttle crew? Do you and your classmates support the idea of space exploration? Why or why not?

4. How successful is the United States' space exploration program? Consider its success in terms of completed missions and the stated purposes for traveling to space.

5. Do you have the desire to travel in outer space? Why or why not? Do you believe the day will come when people will travel in space for recreation and vacation? Why or why not?

Selection 3

DISCOVER WHAT YOU KNOW

1. What is a concentration camp? What groups of people, periods in history, and places have been associated with concentration camps?

2. What have you learned about life in a concentration camp from your study of history and other readings?

3. Where is Argentina? What do you know about the country's politics?

4. What were the political conditions in South America and Central America during the late 1970s?

5. Have the political conditions in South America and Central America changed since the late 1970s?

PREVIEWING

Preview the selection, using your course log and what you have learned from other previewing selections. Write notes in your course log. List the questions you have. Tell what you expect to read about in the selection.

from *THE LITTLE SCHOOL: TALES OF DISAPPEARANCE & SURVIVAL*

Introduction

In the summer of 1984, after four and a half years in **exile,** I returned to my homeland to mourn my friends who had disappeared or were killed by the military, to mourn the members of my family who had died during my **ordeal** of seven years in prison and **banishment,** and to suffer at the sight of my country ruined after years of dictatorship.

Almost 30,000 Argentines "disappeared" between 1976 and 1979, the most oppressive years of the military rule . . . .

On January, 12, 1977, at noon, I was **detained** by uniformed Army personnel at my home, Canadá Street 240, Apt. 2, Bahía Blanca; minutes later the same military personnel detained my husband at his place of work. I was taken to the headquarters of the 5th Army Corps and from there to a **concentration camp,** which the military **ironically** named the Little School (*La Escuelita*). We had no knowledge of the fate of Ruth, our daughter. From that moment on, for the next five months, my husband and I became two more names on the endless list of disappeared people . . . .

Today, while sharing this part of my experience, I pay tribute to a generation of Argentines lost in an attempt to bring social change and justice. I also pay tribute to the victims of **repression** in Latin America.

20 I knew just one Little School, but throughout our continent there are many "schools" whose professors use the lessons of torture and **humiliation** to teach us to lose the memories of ourselves. Beware: in little schools the boundaries between story and history are so subtle that even I can hardly find them.

Alicia Partnoy, *The Little School.* Copyright © 1998. Reprinted by permission of the publisher, Cleis Press.

A PUZZLE

For a while now I've been trying to recall how Ruth's face looks. I can
25 remember her big eyes, her almost non-existent nose, the shape of her mouth. I recall the texture of her hair, the warmth of her skin. When I try to put it all together, something goes wrong. I just can't remember my daughter's face. It has been two months since I've seen her. I want to believe that she's safe.

30 "Vasca! Do you remember my daughter's face?" I whisper.
"What?"
"I said, do you remember my daughter's face? I can't . . ."
"Of course I do, she's so pretty."
I think I'll turn in my bed; that will help me reorder my thoughts . . . No,
35 it doesn't work. It's funny, 'cause I can recall the things we did together, even when I'm not thinking about them all the time. Rather, I've tried not to remember too much, to avoid crying . . . but right now, I want to imagine her face, to put together the pieces of this puzzle . . .

The other day, after the big rain, the guard brought a puppy to our room.
40 He allowed me to keep it on my bed for awhile. It was playful and sweet, like my baby. I felt so good that afternoon that I wanted to laugh. It was not like the **urge** to laugh that I experience when I'm nervous or when I use **black humor** to shield myself. It was a feeling almost close to happiness. While **caressing** the puppy, I thought of Ruth. Then, I didn't worry about
45 trying to remember her face; I just wanted to **reminisce** about being close to her, to recall that warm **tingling** in my blood.

Perhaps if I tried to bring to mind some scenes when we were together . . . For example, that day while coming back from my parents: I was pushing her stroller along the street, when suddenly she looked up at the roof of a house.
50 An immense dog was impatiently **stalking** back and forth. Ruth pointed to the dog with her little finger. "Meow," she said, since she was only used to watching cats climb up high. Thrilled, I kissed her; that kiss was a prize I awarded myself for such a display of wisdom by my child. I stopped the stroller to kiss her . . . but how did her face look? I can only remember her
55 small triumphant smile.

Night is coming; somebody stepped into the room to turn on the lights. We were told that we could take a shower today, but it looks like we're out of luck. It makes me so angry. I shouldn't believe the guards' promises.

The radio is on, not very loud this time . . . playing Roberto Carlos' song
60 again. When the newscast starts, they turn the radio off.

One morning while on the bus I heard on the radio:

"Fellow citizens, if you notice family groups traveling at odd hours of the day or night, report them to the military authorities. The number to call is . . ."

I was one of a few passengers on that early bus. It was 6:30 A.M. and I
65 was traveling to a suburban neighborhood with my baby and two bags. For a short while I thought the driver was going to stop the vehicle and run to the nearest phone to alert the army. He just glared at my reflection in the rear view mirror. The night before some friends of mine had been kidnapped. Since they knew where I lived, I thought of moving out for a few days just to
70 be safe . . . But I can't remember my daughter's face on that bus. I know that she was wearing the pink jacket, that I had the bag with stripes, the same one my mom used to take to the beach. I have perfect recall of every item in the bag . . . but I try so hard and still I can't remember my daughter's face. I could describe her toys, her clothes . . . If only I had her picture. But again, maybe it's
75 better this way. If I could look at a picture of her face, I would surely cry . . . and if I cry, I crumble.

Alicia Partnoy, *The Little School*. Copyright © 1998. Reprinted by permission of the
publisher, Cleis Press.

GLOSSARY

banishment (n.) having been forced to leave a place by official decree

black humor (n.) the blend of depressing elements and comical ones to shock and surprise others

caress (v.) to touch or stroke fondly

concentration camp (n.) a camp where prisoners of war, enemies, and political prisoners are confined

detain (v.) to keep in custody or confinement

exile (n.) enforced removal or self-imposed absence from one's native country

humiliation (n.) degradation; a sense of lowered pride, dignity, and self respect

ironically (adv.) performed in a way showing a difference between what is expected and what actually occurs

reminisce (v.) to recollect and retell the past

repression (n.) the act of removing thoughts from the conscious mind, often through force or brainwashing

stalk (v.) to move in a threatening or menacing way

tingling (adj.) having a prickling, stinging sensation, as from cold or excitement

urge (n.) desire

QUICK COMPREHENSION CHECK ☑

Reread the selection carefully to understand the controlling idea, main points, and most important details. Mark this information when you read, or take notes in your course log. Using your own words and writing in complete sentences, give the highlights of the selection in a brief summary paragraph.

_____

_____

_____

_____

_____

_____

_____

_____

_____

_____

_____

_____

QUESTIONS FOR THOUGHT AND DISCUSSION

1. What was the Little School? How did the name for this place differ from the purpose it served in Argentina, as described by Alicia Partnoy?

2. What happened to Alicia Partnoy on January 12, 1977? Was her experience unusual, or was it one that had become common in her country at that time?

3. Who were Alicia's immediate family members? What happened to them on that same day?

4. Why were the military involved in Alicia's arrest? Although she does not give reasons for her arrest, what is your guess? What are the possible reasons for Alicia's arrest?

5. What memories does Alicia recall in this selection? Who is at the center of her memories? Why? What information does she remember and try to recall frequently?

6. What puzzle is Alicia trying to solve? Why might this puzzle exist?

7. What fears did Alicia live with, both before her arrest and during the time she was at the Little School?

8. What emotions does Alicia express in this selection? Where do you find evidence of these emotions? What do these emotions tell about her?

   Do you regard Alicia as a strong or a weak individual? Why?

9. Why did Alicia write "The Little School"? Who would read this story and material similar to it? What would these readers learn from this type of material?

ANOTHER LOOK AT THE SELECTION

Marking Text

Review the selection to identify parts that were either clear or confusing to you as a reader. Try to understand why the sections appear strong or weak by marking the selection.

1. Scan the selection with a pencil in hand.

2. Mark any part that is confusing with a minus (–) sign; mark any section that is clear with a plus (+) sign.

3. Examine the number of plus and minus signs you have; circle one of the following as a general statement about your comprehension of the selection.

    a. Most of the selection was clear and comprehensible.

    b. Most of the selection was unclear and confusing.

    c. The selection was clear in some parts and confusing in others.

4. a. Which paragraphs or parts were clear and comprehensible?

    1. _____
    2. _____
    3. _____
    4. _____

   b. Explain why these sections were clear to you (consider the vocabulary, the subject matter, writing style, detail and explanation, connecting words, and so on).

    1. _____
    2. _____
    3. _____
    4. _____

5. a. Which paragraphs or parts were unclear or difficult to comprehend?

    1. _____
    2. _____
    3. _____
    4. _____

b. Explain why you found these paragraphs or parts difficult to comprehend.

1. _____

2. _____

3. _____

4. _____

c. What do you think you can do to improve your reading comprehension? Think of all possible strategies: building vocabulary, rereading the material, discussing the material with a classmate, meeting with a tutor, and so on.

1. _____

2. _____

3. _____

4. _____

LOOKING BEYOND THE SELECTION

Concentration Camps

Concentration camps have been part of the human experience in many parts of the world throughout time. Stories from survivors of concentration campus describe the living conditions and horrors. These stories also generate questions about why the camps existed and why certain groups of people persecuted other groups. Learn more about this aspect of history by doing the following:

Children imprisoned at the Nazi concentration camp in Auswitz, Poland.

1. Obtain information about concentration camps on the Internet, in the library, through contact with individuals with firsthand knowledge, through a visit to a museum, or through videos, documentaries, and films.

2. Review the material you chose. Look for background information and photographs that may further orient you to the topic.

3. Seek information of a broad scope; that is, look for information about concentration camps in different parts of the world during various time periods. Aim to learn about four different types of concentration camps.

4. Examine your material; continue to refer to it as you complete the following chart, then answer the questions that follow it.

NAME OF CAMP				
LOCATION				
TIME PERIOD				
CAMP AUTHORITIES				
THE PRISONERS				

5. What new information did you obtain in your search for information about concentration camps?

6. Did the location of any of the concentration camps surprise you? Which ones? Why?

7. For what reasons or circumstances have certain groups of people been sent to concentration camps during the history of the world?

8. Do concentration camps exist anywhere in the world today? Where? Why?

9. People have survived life in the concentration camps, as Alicia Partnoy did. How did they cope with the experience? What human qualities and strengths have enabled them to go on with their lives?

VOCABULARY BUILDING

A Psychological Explanation of the Puzzle

psychology (n.) the science that deals with mental processes and behavior

If you were taking a psychology course right now, you would be studying a number of cases like Alicia's. You would read case histories of individuals and study the different ways in which they reacted to the stresses and traumas in their lives. You also would learn the psychological terms for these reactions.

The following is a list of basic psychological terms for different human reactions to stressful conditions; build your vocabulary by working with these words:

1. Match each term with the appropriate definition

Terms	Definitions
_____ **1.** hysteria (n.)	**a.** a reaction to a disturbance that involves physical withdrawal and an inability to respond; disengagement
_____ **2.** denial (n.)	
_____ **3.** shock (n.)	**b.** excessive or uncontrollable emotion
_____ **4.** selective recall (n.)	**c.** passive awareness of and submission to a situation
_____ **5.** resignation (n.)	**d.** a refusal to accept what has occurred
	e. a subconscious choice about what to remember and what not to remember

2. Which of the previous terms best describes Alicia's puzzling experience?

_____

3. What evidence from the selection supports your answer? What could have happened to Alicia had she seen her daughter's face in her thoughts and memories?

_____

_____

_____

_____

_____

4. How did this puzzling experience actually help Alicia cope with life in the Little School?

_____

_____

_____

_____

_____

_____

IN YOUR WORDS

Choose one or more of the following activities to practice expressing yourself in writing, to understand people's ability to cope, and to explore the human challenges that require the ability to cope. In a brief presentation, share your work with your peers.

1. Keep a double-entry journal for one week. Focus exclusively on life challenges during this time. On one side of the journal, list the life challenges that you experience, observe, or read about. On the other side, record your thoughts on how people who face these challenges attempt to cope.

2. Converse informally with someone who has experienced firsthand the political conditions or imprisonment that Alicia Partnoy described. Write a summary of what you learned from this conversation.

3. Read parts of a story about or diary of someone who experienced life in a concentration camp. In your course log, summarize what you learn. Explain how the material you read is similar to and/or different from the selection's content.

SUMMING UP

Share your thoughts about the selection in a group or with the class. What do others think?

1. How did the class react to Alicia's situation, particularly her separation from her daughter?

2. What is the puzzle the author contemplates? What is the relationship between the puzzle and Alicia's effort to cope with life in the Little School?

3. What different concentration camps did you and your classmates learn about? Where were these camps located? Why did they exist?

4. How did this selection enhance your understanding of how people cope with tragedy and destruction?

5. Imagine the reunion between Alicia and her daughter, Ruth. What emotions would describe that moment in time?

CLOSING THE CHAPTER

Examine the connection between the chapter's two key words—*tragedy* and *coping*—by recording information and ideas in a double-entry journal, as follows:

TRAGEDY AND COPING

WHAT THE AUTHORS DESCRIBE	MY IDEAS
On this side, list chilling details from the three selections, as described by the authors.	On this side, tell how the victims must have felt and how they tried to cope with their circumstances.

Think about the information above. In your course log, write a summary of your thoughts about the human ability to cope.

REFLECTING AND SYTHESIZING

Group Work: Brainstorming

Think about and discuss the different situations people cope with on a day-to-day basis and categorize these situations in some way. For example, you can examine situations at home, at work, at school, or in the community. List the different situations you discuss in your course log.

Next, talk about the broad range of coping skills people need to handle these different situations. In your course log, list your ideas to questions like these:

What are the different ways in which people can cope with difficult circumstances?

What human qualities do people demonstrate when they cope?

Continue your discussion by exploring how coping skills and the human qualities associated with them develop. Record what you and your classmates say in your course log.

Individual Work: Tell Your Story

What times in your life have "tried your soul"? Where were you? How old were you? What happened? How did you react? What was the outcome? What did you learn from this experience? Tell about the most difficult time in your life thus far in an entry to your course log. Depending on your comfort level with the material you write, share some or all of what you write at an appropriate point in your class discussion about this chapter.

5
EXPLORING STRANGE
EVENTS

OPENING THOUGHT

When men and women lose the sense of mystery,
life will prove to be a gray and dreary business,
only with difficulty to be endured.

Harold T. Wilkins
Strange Mysteries of Time and Space (1958)

Think about the chapter's title, quotation, and opening photograph. Answer the following questions:

1. What strange and mysterious events do you know about? How did you learn about them?

_____

_____

_____

2. Do you think the stories about these strange and mysterious events are true? If so, tell why. If not, explain why the stories exist.

_____

_____

_____

3. What do you see in the opening photograph for this chapter? How is it strange and mysterious?

_____

_____

_____

4. Why would life be dreary without stories about strange and mysterious events?

_____

_____

5. What do you expect to read about in this chapter? Do you have any preconceived ideas about the chapter's topic and the types of stories that probably follow?

_____

_____

_____

The selections in this chapter focus on events that fall outside the range of normal activity. Including topics like ghosts and contact with the dead, the stories and accompanying exercises offer you the opportunity to both practice your language skills and question the paranormal.

Selection 1

DISCOVER WHAT YOU KNOW

1. Have you lost someone special? Do you desire to meet with that person once again? Explain.

2. If you were to have contact with this special person one more time, what would you want to discuss with him or her? Why?

3. Tell about the experiences of people you know who claim to have had contact with the dead or who believe contact with the dead is possible.

4. What do you know about different religions or cultures that accept or reject the idea of an afterlife?

PREVIEWING

Preview the selection. Write notes in your course log. List the questions you have and tell what you expect to read about in the selection

BACKGROUND INFORMATION: *Reunions,* by Dr. Raymond Moody, offers many stories about people who believe they had contact with the dead. A medical doctor and a psychologist, Dr. Moody has developed tools such as apparition mirrors for helping people establish this contact. Few people have contact with the dead during a session with Dr. Moody, yet afterwards they encounter their loved ones in familiar places. Dr. Moody feels that contact with a departed relative or friend is part of the healing and mourning process, especially for those individuals who lost someone suddenly or had a lingering conflict with the person who passed away. The following excerpt tells about one person's experience both in the *apparition booth* [a small, enclosed room with a mirror designed to stimulate contact with the dead] and through an *out-of-mirror* experience.

from *REUNIONS: VISIONARY ENCOUNTERS WITH DEPARTED LOVED ONES*

When I was in there [the apparition booth], I kept thinking that I saw something off to my right in the mirror. When I looked at the mirror and tried to focus, the image disappeared. Then I started **gazing** again, and I saw something that looked like it was at my right shoulder. When I turned to

5   look, it was gone. It did look like a person, but I couldn't tell who it was.

Then I saw another image. I knew it was a man, but I had no feeling whatsoever as to who it was. In fact at first I thought it was you [Dr. Raymond Moody] coming in to check on me.

This man was both in and out of the mirror. He **emerged,** and that's why

10   I turned and looked to my right. This was not like a **reflection.** It was a real form coming out of the mirror, but when I turned to look again, it was gone.

At that point I gave up. I came downstairs and was real disappointed because I thought it didn't work.

Then I went home. That first night I started having the **distinct** feeling

15   that someone was around. I would go to sleep, and it was as though I felt someone in the room. I would wake up still feeling that someone had been in there with me, but I couldn't figure out who it was.

On the second night I woke up and had a strong sense of the presence of my father in the room. I could tell that he was trying to talk to me, but I

20   couldn't tell what he was saying. After waking up that time I couldn't go back to sleep.

The next night it happened again. This was the third night in a row in which I went to sleep and woke up feeling a presence in the room. This time I woke up and smelled my father's aftershave lotion.

25 I was completely awake, and this was not a dream, it was very concrete, very here and now.

I looked up, and my father was standing at the door of my bedroom. I had been lying on the bed but I stood up and walked over to him. I was within four steps of him. He looked just like my dad, but not sickly like he had been just before he died. He was full figure, but he looked more fleshed **30** out than when he died. He looked whole, like everything was wonderful.

I didn't hear his voice, but I understood what he was saying. He didn't want me to worry. I got the distinct impression that he was telling me that everything was okay.

I had been very bothered because my dad had died by himself. There was **35** nobody there, and there were a lot of problems at the time of his death, like questions about whether he'd had enough oxygen to make it through the night. That bothered me badly because I am the only child and my mom and dad were separated.

But seeing him that night, I really got the distinct impression that he was **40** okay and that he was telling me that I shouldn't worry about him, that everything was fine. I just knew his thoughts and he knew mine.

And then he just went away. I was awake for quite a while after that. I felt as though I had really been in his presence, and I didn't want to lose that.

From *Reunions* by Dr. Raymond Moody. Copyright © 1993 by Dr. Raymond Moody.
Reprinted by permission of Villard Books, a Division of Random House, Inc.

GLOSSARY

distinct (adj.) clear

emerge (v.) to appear

gaze (v.) to look intently; to stare

reflection (n.) an image given back from a mirror

QUICK COMPREHENSION CHECK ✓

Review the selection carefully to understand the controlling idea, main points, and most important details. Mark this information or write notes in your course log. Use this information to write a brief summary paragraph about the selection.

_____

_____

_____

_____

_____

_____

_____

_____

_____

_____

_____

_____

QUESTIONS FOR THOUGHT AND DISCUSSION

1. Think about the concept of an apparition booth. What might it look like? Would you enter one?

2. Separate and describe the narrator's experience in the apparition booth and her experience at home. How and why do they differ?

3. Summarize what occurred during the narrator's three nights at home.

4. What scent did the narrator smell when she sensed a presence in the room?

5. Who appeared to the narrator?

6. What do you know about the narrator's relationship with this person?

7. How did the narrator feel after having contact with her deceased loved one?

8. Do you accept the narrator's story, or do you doubt it? Explain and support your response.

9. If you do not believe an encounter with the dead occurred, provide an alternate explanation for the narrator's story.

ANOTHER LOOK AT THE SELECTION

Opinion and Support

A variety of opinions about visionary encounters exists. Some individuals are skeptical about them; others accept the concept of visionary encounters fully. What is your opinion? How do you support your opinion?

1. Do you believe the visionary encounter described in the selection actually took place? Circle one response.

    Yes   No

2. Which lines provide support for your belief? Look at both the details provided and the way they are reported. Examine the strength of the words used, including the verbs and pronouns. Consider whether they are definite and specific or vague and weak. Enter the information that supports your opinion into the table on the following page.

LINES (give numbers)	SUPPORTING INFORMATION

3. What personal beliefs support your opinion?

_____

_____

_____

_____

4. Share your work for this exercise with your peers. What different opinions did your group members express?

_____

_____

_____

_____

_____

LOOKING BEYOND THE SELECTION

Why might you need to obtain more information about visionary encounters? Where would you look for this information? Working independently or in a group, search for more information about the experience of sensing the presence of or meeting with a deceased person.

You can use a number of terms to do your search: *visionary encounters, extrasensory perception,* and the *paranormal.* Try to find a variety of stories about visionary encounters—stories from different time periods and different places.

A. Use different approaches for finding this information, from traditional library approaches to electronic searches on the Internet. List the sources for the information you found.

    1. _____

    2. _____

    3. _____

    4. _____

B. Try to keep your study of the topic balanced. Find stories about visionary encounters as well as the words of the skeptics who doubt that visionary encounters take place. What do skeptics say? What explanation do they give for someone who claims a visionary encounter has taken place?

1. Share what you read with a group or the entire class. Has anyone's opinion about visionary encounters changed through this research project? Explain.

_____

_____

_____

_____

2. Tell whether your sources provided valid information about the topic.

_____

_____

_____

VOCABULARY BUILDING

The narrator tells how the *image* of her father appeared during the visionary encounter. Look up the word *image* in a dictionary. Think about how it is unique in contrast to similar words, such as the word *ghost.* Then circle all the words in the following list that could substitute for the word *image* in the selection:

body	presence	shadow
reflection	specter	picture
impression	character	figure
mirror	likeness	idea

After completing the exercise, you may be uncertain about whether some words would or would not substitute for the word *image.* Write your thoughts about the points of confusion in your course log. Present your ideas for class discussion at an appropriate time.

IN YOUR WORDS

Have you ever walked into a room or experienced an event and had the feeling that you had experienced the situation before? When alone, especially on a dark, stormy night, do you ever feel your skin bristle as though it is responding to some presence? How do you feel when the lights go out and you are alone in the dark? At times like these, you may have an unexplained feeling or sense a presence in your midst.

Freewrite here; tell whether you have experienced the strange or paranormal or tell why you doubt that experiences of this type actually exist.

_____

_____

_____

_____

_____

_____

_____

_____

_____

_____

_____

_____

Share what you wrote with your peers.

SUMMING UP

Share your thoughts about the selection in a group or with the class. What do others think?

1. What different opinions did you and your classmates express about the visionary encounter described in this selection?

2. Have you, your classmates, or someone you know ever experienced a visionary encounter? Who experienced the visionary encounter? When? What happened? Why did the visionary encounter take place?

3. How does a visionary encounter differ from a religious experience in which a sacred person or object appears to an individual or group of people?

4. What different visionary encounters did you and your classmates learn about? Do you and your classmates believe that visionary encounters occur, or do you believe an alternate explanation for what people claim exists? Tell about the supporting arguments believers use; tell about the supporting arguments skeptics use.

5. Would you and your classmates welcome a visionary encounter, or would you fear contact with a deceased person? What reasons do people cite for their reactions to the possibility of having an encounter with the dead?

Selection 2

DISCOVER WHAT YOU KNOW

1. Tell the ghost stories you know. What is the origin or source for these stories? Do you believe them?

2. What do you know about ghosts and the Halloween custom in the United States? Do you have a custom or practice in your country that is similar?

3. What do people from your country believe about ghosts? Why?

4. What places in your country are believed to be haunted or visited by ghosts?

PREVIEWING

Preview the selection. Write notes in your course log. List the questions you have and tell what you expect to read about in the selection.

BACKGROUND INFORMATION: As President of the Ghost Club, Peter Underwood takes stories about ghosts seriously. He has seen many ghosts because he visits those places where ghosts are said to be present. Mr. Underwood feels that ghosts revisit places where they used to live or go because they have work to do there—they may have to solve lingering problems or intervene to prevent expected crises. The purpose of Mr. Underwood's research is to gather evidence of a ghost's appearance—perhaps a photograph of an image or consistent eyewitness accounts of sightings. One of his stories follows. It is actually two stories in one. In the first part, Mr.Underwood tells about the appearance of the Brown Lady in 1835. The second part focuses on his personal experience with the Brown Lady in 1936, as shown in the accompanying photograph.

THE BROWN LADY

from *GHOSTS AND HOW TO SEE THEM*

With or without the somewhat **vague** photograph, taken in 1936, the ghostly Brown Lady of Raynham Hall, Fakenham, Norfolk, near the east coast of England, seat of the **marquess** of Townshend, has reportedly been seen on many occasions over the past 150 years. Many reports involve a
5   figure moving quietly down the main staircase, along one of the **corridors,** and in and out of one of the first-floor bedrooms; a clear and distinct figure seemingly dressed in a gown of brown satin with yellow trimmings and a ruff around the throat. The features are quite clearly defined but the eyes are sometimes dark **hollows** and her cheeks have been described as unnaturally
10   white. She is usually silent and harmless, but very occasionally there seems to be an evil, **menacing** quality about the **haunting** figure and sightings of her have been known to bring terror to those who experience them. This reaction may well rest with the witness and have nothing to do with the ghostly figure. . . .
15   [O]ne of the well-attested sightings of the famous Brown Lady occurred when Captain Frederick Marryat (1792–1848) came to stay. . . . This knowledgeable and honest seaman always claimed to have encountered the Brown Lady during a visit to Raynham Hall in 1835, when he was among the guests of Lord and Lady Charles Townshend.
20   His host talked of reported sightings of the ghost and Marryat told his friend not to be upset by such tales. He said he did not believe in ghosts and if somebody was playing tricks he would welcome the opportunity of crossing swords with them!

25 Marryat occupied a large, first-floor, panelled room, containing a portrait of Dorothy Walpole, whose ghost the Brown Lady is thought to be. She was a direct blood relative of the Townshends, who lived unhappily at Raynham Hall suffering mental depression and spending the last years of her life **confined** to that particular room. Her brother was Sir Robert Walpole, England's Prime Minister in 1722. The sad Dorothy is supposed to be

30 looking for her children, who had been taken away from her when she and her husband separated. There have also been stories that she either fell or was pushed to her death down the staircase that her ghost now haunts.

Before settling down for the night Marryat took the precaution of placing a loaded revolver under his pillow. The first night passed without incident, as

35 did the second night, and the third night—except that just as he was about to **retire,** two nephews of Lord Charles Townshend, who were sharing a bedroom further down the corridor, asked him whether he would be good enough to give them his opinion on a new gun one of them had bought. The captain agreed, picked up a candle and, as an **afterthought,** took his loaded

40 revolver and followed the two young men to their bedroom.

Having seen the gun and **duly** admired it Marryat prepared to return to his own room. The two young men said they would see him back there, so the three set off down the gloomy corridor together, only their footfalls breaking the silence of the quiet old house. They had gone only a few steps

45 when the captain **halted.** 'Look. . .' he whispered. Moving towards them from the direction of Marryat's room was the figure of a woman, wearing a dress that **rustled** as she walked.

As the figure approached all three men noticed the temperature drop and Captain Marryat saw that the features of the figure closely resembled the

50 portrait in his bedroom while the clothing matched that described to him by Lord Townshend. Thinking this must be someone playing at being the ghost he pointed his revolver at the figure, but it made no difference, and waiting until the figure was within feet of him, Captain Marryat fired his revolver **point-blank** at it! The noise in the confined space of the corridor was

55 deafening and the three men waited for the smoke to clear, expecting to see a body . . . but the corridor was completely deserted. They all felt it might have been a **hallucination** except that their description tallied and a bullet hole in the panelling of the corridor showed where the captain's bullet had gone through the figure they all had seen. . . .

◆ ◆ ◆ ◆ ◆ ◆ ◆ ◆

60 Some years ago a correspondent, Mrs. Gladys Marshall of South Harrow, wrote to inform me that she had attended a school at West Raynham and for as long as she could remember all the children knew about the Brown Lady. . . .

She informed me that it was the Dowager Manchioress Townshend who had agreed to some photographers visiting Raynham Hall in 1936. She was interested in the subject of ghosts and quite fascinated by the resulting photograph. It was arranged that two top professional photographers, Captain Provand, art director of a Piccadilly firm of Court photographers, and his assistant Indre Shira, would visit the Hall and take photographs for *Country Life* magazine. On the morning of 19 September 1936 they duly arrived and took a large number of photographs of the house and grounds and then, at about four o'clock in the afternoon, they came to the oak staircase. Indre Shira described what happened next in *Country Life* dated December 1936.

Captain Provand took one photograph of it while I flashed the light. He was focusing again for another exposure; I was standing by his side just behind the camera with the flashlight pistol in my hand, looking directly up the staircase.

The ghost of the Brown Lady, on the staircase in Raynham Hall in 1936

All at once I detected an **ethereal,** veiled form coming slowly down the stairs. Rather excitedly I called out sharply: 'Quick! Quick! There's
80 something! Are you ready?' 'Yes' the photographer replied, and removed the cap from the lens. I pressed the trigger of the flashlight pistol. After the flash, and on the closing shutter, Captain Provand removed the focusing cloth from his head and, turning to me, said: 'What's all the excitement about?'

85 I directed attention to the staircase and explained that I had distinctly seen a figure there—**transparent** so that the steps were visible through the ethereal form, but nevertheless very definite and to me perfectly real. He laughed and said I must have imagined I had seen a ghost—for there was nothing now to be seen. It may be of interest to record that the flash from the
90 Sasha bulb, which in this instance was used, is equivalent, I understand, to a speed of one-fiftieth part of a second. . . .

When the negatives of Raynham Hall were developed, I stood beside Captain Provand in the dark-room. One after the other they were placed in the developer. Suddenly Captain Provand exclaimed: 'Good Lord! There's
95 something on the staircase negative, after all!' I took one glance, called to him 'Hold it' and dashed downstairs to the chemist, Mr. Benjamin Jones, manager of Blake, Sandford and Blake, whose premises are immediately underneath our studio. I invited Mr. Jones to come upstairs to our dark-room. He came, and saw the negative just as it had been taken from the developer
100 and placed in the adjoining hypo bath. Afterwards, he declared that, had he not seen for himself the negative being fixed, he would not have believed in the genuineness of the picture. Incidentally, Mr. Jones has had considerable experience as an **amateur** photographer in developing his own plates and films.

105 Mr. Jones, Captain Provand and I vouch for the fact that the negative has not been retouched in any way. It has been examined critically by a number of experts. No one can account for the appearance of the ghostly figure; but it is there clear enough. . . .

From Peter Underwood, *Ghosts and How to See Them,* London: Anaya Publishers, Ltd. Copyright © 1993.

GLOSSARY

afterthought (n.) an idea that occurs to a person after an event or decision

amateur (adj.) pertaining to a person who engages in an activity as a pastime and not as a profession

confine (v.) to restrict; to imprison

corridor (n.) a narrow hall or passageway, often with rooms opening onto it

duly (adv.) in a proper manner; at the expected time

ethereal (adj.) delicate; heavenly

hallucination (n.) a false or mistaken idea; a delusion

halt (v.) to stop

haunting (adj.) visiting or appearing in the form of a ghost or spirit

hollow (n.) a cavity or inner space; an indented surface

marquess (n.) the wife of a nobleman

menacing (adj.) troublesome, annoying, or threatening

point-blank (adj.) aiming straight at a target

retire (v.) to withdraw, as for rest or seclusion; to go to bed

rustle (v.) to move or cause to move with soft fluttering or crackling sounds

transparent (adj.) transmitting light so objects on the other side can be seen

vague (adj.) lacking definite shape, form, or character

QUICK COMPREHENSION CHECK ✔

Reread the selection carefully to understand the controlling idea, main points, and most important details. Mark this information when you read, or take notes in your course log. Using your own words and writing in complete sentences, give the highlights of the selection in a brief summary paragraph.

_____

_____

_____

_____

_____

_____

_____

_____

QUESTIONS FOR THOUGHT AND DISCUSSION

1. Where has the Brown Lady appeared? Since when? How is she usually dressed when she appears?

2. What do you know about the lady's facial features and expression? Would you say she is a "good" ghost or a "bad" ghost?

3. Summarize the "well-attested" sighting of the Brown Lady that is the focus of the first part of the selection. Who saw the Brown Lady? Where? When?

   Explain how a gun provided evidence of the Brown Lady's appearance.

4. What happened to the room temperature when the ghostly figure appeared? Why do you think this happened?

5. What background information about the Brown Lady does the selection provide? What is her name? Her family history? Her personal story?

6. What reasons might the Brown Lady have for returning to this house?

7. What is the connection between the author of the story and the Brown Lady?

8. Summarize what Indu Shira wrote about the Brown Lady in *Country Life* magazine in 1936.

9. Did Mr. Jones, Captain Provand, and the author provide sufficient evidence of the Brown Lady's appearance as a ghost?

10. What explanations, other than the appearance of a ghost, might exist for what the author describes in the selection?

ANOTHER LOOK AT THE SELECTION

Examining Evidence

This selection does more than tell a ghost story. It includes information about attempts to document and authenticate the ghost's appearance. People are more likely to accept accounts of paranormal events if they can see physical evidence of their occurrence.

A. Before examining the evidence, develop working definitions for the two key verbs in this exercise: *document* and *authenticate*. Write the following:

1. **to document** (v.)

   Dictionary definition _____

   _____

Your working definition _____

_____

_____

2. to authenticate (v.)

Dictionary definition _____

_____

Your working definition _____

_____

_____

B. Identify and evaluate evidence from the selection. Does it document and authenticate the presence of a ghost? Consider supporting details for the following:

1. The sighting in 1835

Physical evidence _____

_____

_____

Is the evidence sufficient to document the presence of a ghost?

     Yes   No

2. The photograph taken in the 1930s.

Witnesses _____

_____

_____

Is the evidence sufficient to document the presence of a ghost?

     Yes   No

LOOKING BEYOND THE SELECTION

A. Information in lines 24–32 suggests that the Brown Lady had reasons for returning to Raynham Hall. Reread the paragraph and list those reasons.

1. _____

2. _____

3. _____

4. _____

5. _____

B. Look beyond the selection to learn what experts on ghosts say to explain their appearance. Work with your peers to organize your work for this part. Search the Internet, library, and other information available to find reasons why ghosts appear. List the reasons you find.

1. _____

2. _____

3. _____

4. _____

5. _____

VOCABULARY BUILDING

Some boldface words from the selection and other new words appear in this exercise on words associated with the appearance of ghosts. By discussing the words with your peers and using a dictionary, match the words and their definitions.

Vocabulary

_____ **1.** menacing (adj.)

_____ **2.** haunting (adj.)

_____ **3.** phantom (adj.)

_____ **4.** ethereal (adj.)

_____ **5.** transparent (adj.)

_____ **6.** seance (n.)

Meanings

a. delicate; heavenly

b. a meeting or sitting to receive spiritual messages

c. troublesome; threatening

d. unreal; ghostlike

e. continually recurring; unforgettable

f. obvious; capable of being seen through

IN YOUR WORDS

Add to Your Opinion

In other sections, you started to explore your opinion about the chapter's topics. Continue to develop your opinion by writing about **one** of the following questions. Consider your outside reading, if you wish. Write your response in your course log. Be prepared to share what you think with a partner, in a group, or with your class.

1. Why do ghosts appear?

2. What are normal explanations for what others erroneously call the appearance of ghosts?

3. Why are ghost stories common?

4. Why do some people enjoy telling ghost stories?

5. What age group tends to enjoy ghost stories more than any other age group?

6. Why are some ghosts good?

7. Why are some ghosts bad?

8. Why would films, artwork, or literature feature ghosts?

SUMMING UP

Share your thoughts about the selection in a group or with the class. What do others think?

1. Do you and your classmates believe that the Brown Lady actually appeared in Raynham Hall? Are your opinions the same or different? If disagreement exists, summarize some of the points of disagreement.

2. What do you and your classmates think about the photograph of the Brown Lady? Is the image on the stairs really the Brown Lady? What other explanations might exist for the image on the staircase?

3. What do you and your classmates know about ghosts? How are ghosts different from a visionary encounter, as described in the preceding selection? Are the two phenomena the same or different? Why?

4. How do you and your classmates feel about the idea that ghosts have reasons for appearing? What reasons in your research offer the most plausible explanation for why ghosts might appear?

Selection 3

DISCOVER WHAT YOU FEEL

1. Do you believe that certain events or situations are signs that direct the decisions we make and the actions we take? Explain and provide examples.

2. Have you or someone you know seen or felt an event take place before it actually occurred? Was this event a good event or a bad event? Explain.

3. Do you believe people can see the future?

4. How powerful is the human mind? What might interfere with someone's ability to use his or her mind to its full potential?

PREVIEWING

Preview the selection. Write notes in your course log. List the questions you have and tell what you expect to read about in the selection.

BACKGROUND INFORMATION: Rosalind Heywood, the author of this selection, is said to have six senses. Along with the ability to see, taste, feel, hear, and smell, she knows about events before they take place and senses a special role she must play in some of these events. Mrs. Heywood's abilities, which extend beyond the normal, show that she has ESP, Extrasensory Perception. In her autobiography, *ESP: A Personal Memoir,* she tells the story that follows. It focuses on a time when she sensed warnings about the future and the need to go on a special mission. Elsewhere in her autobiography, Mrs. Heywood tells how her special missions for other people often have nothing to do with a close relationship with them but, rather, with her paranormal mental abilities to receive messages and pass these messages on to others.

from *ESP: A PERSONAL MEMOIR*

At parties we [the author and her husband] often met a beautiful and **seductive** woman called Julia, who was also kind hearted in the nicest American way. We both felt drawn to her for she made us laugh, but a soap bubble would have **counter-weighed** any talk we had together [their conversation was light, not serious]. One hot summer's day Julia and I were **idling** with some friends round the swimming pool of a millionaire. No one appeared to have a thought in the world beyond enjoying the sun which **dappled** our **mahogany** bodies through the trees. Suddenly she thrust out

5

her hands. 'Read them for me,' she said. . . .
Laughing, I took her hands and looked at
them, and then heard myself saying, very
gravely, 'You will never find what you
are looking for in this world, will you?'

She replied, equally gravely, 'No.'

This startled me. It is
always a shock when
another order of things
erupts, like **Poseidon,** from
a foaming sunlit sea; but this
time, as usual, the foam swept
over it as our care-free friends
surrounded us, and the moment of truth was
gone. A few weeks later Julia gave a farewell cocktail party before flying to
Peru on a visit, and at it she brought me a snapshot of herself, saying, 'This
is for you, Rosalind.'

I made a **futile** cocktail-party reply, 'Oh, surely you mean for Frank?'
(my husband) but she said seriously, 'No, I mean for you.' At that Orders [an
inner voice] said, 'Take it. This is important;' and so I thanked her quietly
and took the snapshot.

A day or two later the news arrived that her plane had crashed in the
Andes with no survivors. Then followed a strange forty-eight hours, which,
whether or not they were **self-induced,** have at least enabled me to
sympathize with people who feel themselves to be **mediums** or even
possessed. I could not get Julia out of my head—not the crash, not any sense
of disaster, just her. Even when driving my car I found myself **muttering** her
name, 'Julia, Julia, Julia!'

This puzzled me. It was not natural. Of course, the news of her death was
a shock, as it always is when someone very much alive suddenly **ceases** to
exist. But much as we liked her, she had in no way been part of our lives, and
my constant thought of her did not make sense. I supposed, however, that the
suddenness of her death had been more of a shock than I had realized.

Two days later, most unusually, I found myself with a free afternoon; no
parties, the servants out, a glorious **pause.** 'I'll just write my **condolences** to
Julia's mother,' I thought, 'and then I'll lie down on the garden room sofa
and do nothing, nothing at all.'

The letter was a **feeble** effort, shy, stiff and **conventional.** I felt ashamed
of it, but could do no better for I hardly knew Julia's mother, I had little in
common with her, and I did not believe that anything of Julia had survived
the destruction of her body. When finished I put it down on my desk with a
sigh of relief and then settled myself on the sofa beside it to enjoy the lovely

peace. I did not enjoy it long. Although our house stood back from the road in a little-used sidestreet and its garden side was utterly quiet, a few minutes later a Viennese woodcut which was hanging at the far side of the desk fell with a sudden crash to the ground. Very puzzled, I ran over and picked it up.

55 It was undamaged and the cord was **intact.** I looked at the nail. It was just as it should be. Then why and how had the woodcut fallen? I was standing by my desk trying to puzzle out this **conundrum** when my eye caught the letter to Julia's mother, and at that inside my head I heard Julia speak. She spoke in no uncertain terms. 'Don't send that silly letter,' she said. 'Go to my

60 mother now, straight away, and tell her to stop all that ridiculous mourning at once. I'm very happy and I can't stand it.'

This sudden **eruption** of the **remote** 'other' caught me quite unawares, but at the moment I had no more doubt that it was Julia conveying to me her urgent wishes than I doubt it when my husband asks me to pass him the

65 honey at breakfast. But I also had no doubt that were I to rush off to Julia's mother with this extraordinary story, my husband being at the British Embassy the town would buzz with talk. The more I hesitated the more insistent 'Julia' became, until at last I rang my husband and said, 'I don't know what to do.' As usual he settled the thing at once. 'Better be a fool than

70 a **knave,**' he said. 'Go, if you feel you ought to.'

At that, feeling indeed every kind of fool, I got out my car and went. What made the situation yet more embarrassing was that at the time I knew nothing of the conventions of Americans from the Southern States in face of death, and ignorantly assumed that Julia's mother would behave like mine in

75 similar circumstances, wear her ordinary clothes and hide her grief under a mask of frozen normality. If this were so, to **barge** in and ask her to stop an **excessive** display of mourning seemed both pointless and rude. However, on arrival at her house I found all the blinds down and in the hall a **covey** of **melancholy** women, talking in whispers and looking like crows. 'May I see

80 Mrs. Howard?' I asked them.

They looked shocked. 'Certainly not,' they said, 'she's in bed, mourning.'

That settled it. 'I must see her,' I insisted, and after much protest they took me up to her room. There, indeed, was the poor woman, alone, in the dark, in bed. Intensely embarrassed, for I supposed this was by her own

85 choice, I got out my message, expecting to be thrown out at once as mad or **impertinent.** But her face lit up. 'I knew it,' she cried, 'I knew she'd hate it, and I didn't want it. I shall get up and stop it at once!'

On me the effect of her response was curious. From that moment all sense of Julia's presence **vanished;** it was as if, content, she had gone off at

90 once on her own affairs, and from then on I thought of her no more than was normal, and certainly with no sorrow. . . .

From *ESP: A Personal Memoir,* by Rosalind Heywood, E.P. Dutton & Company, 1964.

GLOSSARY

barge (v.) to intrude

cease (v.) to stop

condolence (n.) expression of sympathy or sorrow

conundrum (n.) a riddle or dilemma

conventional (adj.) following accepted practice; customary

counter-weigh (v.) to balance

covey (n.) a small flock or group

dapple (v.) to mark or mottle with spots

erupt (v.) to break out violently

eruption (n.) violent outbreak

excessive (adj.) being more than is required

feeble (adj.) lacking strength; weak

futile (adj.) useless

idle (v.) to pass time without working; to move lazily

impertinent (adj.) disrespectfully arrogant

intact (adj.) not impaired in any way

knave (n.) a man who is crafty

mahogany (adj.) reddish-brown

medium (n.) a person thought to have the power to communicate with the spirits of the dead

melancholy (n.) sadness; depression

mutter (v.) to speak or utter indistinctly in low tones

pause (v.) to suspend an action temporarily

Poseidon (n.) in Greek mythology, the brother of Zeus and god of water and earthquakes

remote (adj.) located far away; distant in time

seductive (adj.) raising hope or desire

self-induced (adj.) brought about by oneself

vanish (v.) to disappear

QUICK COMPREHENSION CHECK

Review the selection carefully to understand the controlling idea, main point, and most important details. Mark this information or take notes in your course log. Use the information to construct a brief summary paragraph for the selection.

_____

_____

_____

_____

_____

_____

_____

_____

_____

_____

_____

_____

_____

_____

QUESTIONS FOR THOUGHT AND DISCUSSION

1. Describe Rosalind's and Julia's friendship.

   How deep was this friendship?

   What did the two women tend to do together?

2. Tell about Julia, as you see her through Rosalind's eyes. Is the picture of Julia a flattering one, or does it show her flaws?

3. What is the significance of the photograph Julia gave Rosalind at the cocktail party?

   How did Rosalind react to receiving it?

   What did Julia say when she presented the photograph to Rosalind?

4. What happened to Julia as she traveled to Peru?

   How did Rosalind react to what happened?

5. What took place in Rosalind's house shortly after she finished her note to Julia's mother? Tell about both the Viennese woodcut and the message Rosalind received.

6. What does Rosalind mean by the term *remote other?*

   How is this *remote other* part of the story about her and Julia?

   What does the *remote other* cause Julia to do?

7. What happened when Rosalind saw Mrs. Howard, Julia's mother?

   What was Mrs. Howard's condition?

   How did Rosalind's visit and message affect Mrs. Howard's condition? How did Rosalind feel after she visited Mrs. Howard?

8. Why did Rosalind believe she had to visit Mrs. Howard?

   Do you believe Rosalind's explanation? Tell why or why not.

ANOTHER LOOK AT THE SELECTION

Evaluating the Evidence

Examine details in the story. Were the incidents that appeared strange to Rosalind Heywood really that strange? Use the following double-entry journal as a means to analyze this question:

STRANGE INCIDENT	AN ALTERNATE EXPLANATION
List incidents the author describes as strange here.	Tell why the incident may not be so strange after all. Give another explanation about why or how the incident occurred.

After you complete the double-entry journal, write a position statement about the selection in your course log. Tell whether you do or do not believe the incident to be beyond the range of normal activity. Support your position with information from the journal entry.

LOOKING BEYOND THE SELECTION

In this selection, the author describes one time when her extrasensory perception (ESP) was active. Elsewhere in her book, she describes more episodes. In each, her ability to sense events and emotions beyond space and time are keen. To understand the author's extrasensory perception fully, you need a thorough understanding of the term, which you can acquire by doing the following:

1. Look up the term *extrasensory perception* in a dictionary, in the library, or on the Internet. Write the definition you found.

_____

_____

_____

_____

2. Restate this definition in your own words.

_____

_____

_____

3. Find examples and illustrations that expand your definition. Using the Internet, the library, and other research resources, search for more stories about ESP. List the different extrasensory experiences you read about.

a. _____

b. _____

c. _____

d. _____

e. _____

VOCABULARY BUILDING

The experiences you listed in the preceding section identify some or all of the types of ESP humans can have. Learning about these experiences may not have given you a clear orientation to the term for the different types of ESP. They are listed here, along with their definitions. Using a dictionary, information from your reading, and other resources, match the different types of ESP and their definitions.

Vocabulary	Meanings
_____ 1. clairvoyance	**a.** knowledge of the future
_____ 2. channeling	**b.** the movement of objects that cannot be explained
_____ 3. precognition	**c.** thought transference between people
_____ 4. telekinesis	**d.** the power to see objects or events that cannot be perceived by the senses
_____ 5. psychokinesis	**e.** the process whereby a being communicates through a human
_____ 6. telepathy	**f.** controlling the motion of objects through psychic powers

IN YOUR WORDS

Cross-Cultural Perspectives

1. What do you know about palm reading, crystal balls, fortunetelling, and Ouija Boards™? If you are familiar with these **mediums** for supernatural powers, tell where and how you learned about them. If you are not familiar with these mediums, seek information from a classmate, outside reading material, or your instructor.

   _____

   _____

   _____

   _____

2. Are the mediums mentioned in number 1 used in your culture? By whom? When? Why? Does someone from your country who is interested in the paranormal use other mediums besides the ones mentioned? If so, what are these mediums? What do they look like? How are they used? What information might a person obtain through them?

_____

_____

_____

_____

3. In your country what is the general feeling about the paranormal, such as topics in this chapter and other topics such as aliens from outer space? Is literature on such topics available? Are movies about such topics made?

_____

_____

_____

_____

4. What differences do you find between the way people in the United States and the way people in your country perceive strange and paranormal events? Why do these differences exist?

_____

_____

_____

5. Do you find any connection between religious beliefs and attitudes towards the strange and paranormal?

_____

_____

_____

6. What stories about the strange and the paranormal are popular in your country? How did you, personally, learn about these stories?

_____

_____

_____

_____

7. Share your answers to the preceding questions with a partner, in a group, or in a class discussion. Tell one of the stories from your country. Afterwards, write in your course log a summary of cross-cultural perspectives about the strange and paranormal.

SUMMING UP

Share your thoughts about the selection in a group or with the class. What do others think?

1. How would you and your classmates describe Rosalind? Does she really have special powers?

2. What unusual circumstances or events occur in this story? Are they really that unusual? Are there more normal ways for explaining why these events or circumstances occurred? Do you and your classmates agree that this story is beyond the range of normal experience? Why or why not?

3. What other stories do you and your classmates know about extrasensory perception? Tell about stories from your research and stories from your personal experience. Work to explain the concept of extrasensory perception in your own words.

4. How do you and your classmates think people with ESP feel about their ability to sense knowledge and circumstances in ways beyond the range of normal experience? What are the advantages and disadvantages of having extrasensory powers?

5. Do you and your classmates feel that the Internet is a valid source of information about extrasensory perception and the paranormal?

Selection 4

DISCOVER WHAT YOU KNOW

1. Where is the area known as the Bermuda Triangle?

2. Have you ever traveled to or through this area?

3. What is said to occur in the Bermuda Triangle area? What evidence of these occurrences exists?

4. Which other areas of the world are believed to have the same effect as the Bermuda Triangle may have?

5. What can you do to learn more about the Bermuda Triangle?

PREVIEWING

Preview the selection. Write notes in your course log. List the questions you have and tell what you expect to read about in the selection.

BACKGROUND INFORMATION: Are you familiar with any one of the following places—the State of Florida; San Juan, Puerto Rico; or the Island of Bermuda? Located in the area that runs through the southern part of the Atlantic Ocean to the Caribbean Sea, these three places are considered the points of the Bermuda Triangle, an area where over 50 ships and planes have disappeared in the last two decades. Also known as the Devil's Triangle, the area is believed, by some, to be occupied by UFO's (Unidentified Flying Objects) and extraterrestrial beings that capture aircraft and ships. No scientific evidence supports this belief, yet people are still puzzled by the wreckage in this portion of the Atlantic Ocean. This selection focuses on Flight 19, a team of military aircraft that disappeared in the area known as the Bermuda Triangle. The author provides a detailed account of the team's final hours in the air. Many circumstances and conditions existed on that day, making the fate of Flight 19 a topic of much debate.

FLIGHT 19

from *UNEXPLAINED: 347 STRANGE SIGHTINGS, INCREDIBLE OCCURRENCES AND PUZZLING PHYSICAL PHENOMENA*

The Tragedy.

At 2:10 on the afternoon of December 5, 1945, five Avenger torpedo bombers left the Naval Air Station (NAS) at Fort Lauderdale, Florida, and headed east. Flight 19 was made up of 14 men, all students in the last stages of training except for the commander, Lt. Charles Taylor. The five pilots had been transferred only recently from the Miami Naval Air Station. Taylor knew the Florida Keys well; he did not know the Bahamas, in whose direction he and the others were heading.

The purpose of the exercise was to conduct a practice bombing. . . . Once that was accomplished, the Avengers were to continue eastward for another 67 miles, then head north 73 miles. After that they would turn west-southwest and take the remaining 120 miles straight home. In short, they were flying a triangular flight path through what would be called the Bermuda Triangle.

At 3:40 P.M. a pilot and flight instructor, Lt. Robert Cox, who was about to land at Fort Lauderdale, overheard a radio **transmission** addressed to someone named Powers. Powers replied, "I don't know where we are. We must have got lost after that last turn." Fort Lauderdale attempted to communicate with Powers (in fact Marine Capt. Edwards Powers, Jr.) but got no immediate response. A few minutes later Cox established contact with Taylor, the pilot who had spoken to Powers. The pilot was Lt. Taylor. Taylor told Cox that his compasses were not working, but "I'm sure I'm in the Keys, but . . . I don't know how to get to Fort Lauderdale." Cox urged him to fly north toward Miami "if you are in the Keys."

Taylor was not, however, in the Keys. He was in the Bahamas. By flying north he would only go farther out to sea. Efforts by Cox and others to establish just the location of Flight 19 were **hampered** by poor communications. At one point Taylor was urged to turn over control of the flight to one of the students, though apparently he did not do so; the occasional overheard exchange between him and other Flight 19 pilots suggested some degree of **dissension.** Just after 4:30 P.M. Taylor radioed a question to Port Everglades Boat Facility, and Air Sea Rescue Unit near Fort Lauderdale: "Do you think, as my student does, that we should fly west?" Not knowing where he was, Port Everglades simply **acknowledged** receiving his transmission. If Flight 19 had flown west at this stage, it would have been saved.

At 4:45 P.M. Taylor indicated that the Avengers were going to go north-northeast for a short time, then head north "to make sure we are not over the Gulf of Mexico." By now the people on the ground were seriously concerned; it was clear that Taylor, far from being temporarily lost as happens to many pilots, had no idea where he was. As dusk approached, atmospheric interference with the radio signals increased. Through the static, two of the student pilots could be heard complaining that "if we would just fly west, we would get home." Nonetheless they flew north, then **veered** off slightly to the east, for a few minutes. At 5:15 P.M. Taylor called in to Port Everglades, "We are now heading west." Taylor addressed his companions, telling them that they should join up; as soon as one of them ran out of fuel, they would all go down together.

The sun set at 5:29 P.M. With bad weather moving in from the north, the situation was growing ever more urgent, but no one on the ground knew where Flight 19 was. Around 6:00 P.M. reception improved for a short time. Taylor was urged to switch to 3000 **kilocycles,** the emergency **frequency,** but refused to do so for fear he and the other planes would fall out of communication; unfortunately, interference from Cuban commercial stations and the inability of other coastal stations to translate the Fort Lauderdale training signal easily would effectively shut off Flight 19 from the rest of the world.

A few minutes earlier, at 5:50 P.M., the ComGulf Sea Frontier Evaluation Center thought it had pinpointed the flight's approximate position: east of New Smyrna Beach, Florida, and far to the north of the Bahamas. At 6:04 P.M.

Mysterious wreckage lying on the floor of the waters surrounding Bermuda

Taylor was heard ordering the others to "turn around and go east again." Two minutes later he repeated the order, explaining, "I think we would have a better chance of being picked up." Apparently he still believed the flight was over the Gulf.

So far no rescue aircraft had gone out because the position fix had not yet been passed on to all affected parties, not the least of them Taylor and his companions. But finally a Dumbo flying boat [a cargo plane] based at the Dinner Key seaplane base left Miami, heading northeast, at 6:20 P.M. on what amounted to a blind effort to reestablish contact. The Dumbo itself soon fell out of contact with the shore, however, and for a while it was feared that it, too, was lost. The problem turned out to be icing on the antenna, and the Dumbo continued on what proved to be a **futile** search.

Within the hour other aircraft joined it, including two Martin Mariners (Training 32 and Training 49), the second of which departed from the Banana River NAS at 7:27 P.M. This Mariner was to join up with the first . . . [yet] failed to make its scheduled **rendezvous,** and it was not answering radio calls. At 7:50 P.M. the crew of the *SS Gaines Mill* observed an enormous sheet of fire caused by the explosion of an airplane. A few minutes later the ship passed through a big pool of oil and looked with no success for survivors or bodies. Though they saw some **debris,** crew members did not try **to retrieve** any of it because of the ocean **turbulence.** Weather conditions were **deteriorating** rapidly.

The Flight 19 aircraft now had exhausted their fuel and were assumed to be down. Taylor's last transmission was heard at 7:04 P.M. The search continued through the night, though at a **diminished** rate because of turbulence in the air and on the ocean. The next day hundreds of planes and ships looked **in vain,** on heavy seas, for the missing Avengers and Mariner. No trace of them turned up then, later, or ever. . . .

Myth and mystification.

In September 1950 Associated Press reporter E.V.W. Jones sent a story out on the wires. Its echoes would be heard for decades to come. In it he wrote that a triangular area connecting Florida, Bermuda, and Puerto Rico comprised a "limbo of the lost" where planes and ships often "vanished in the thin air." An especially **baffling** mystery was the disappearance of Flight 19 and the Martin Mariner which had gone in search of it. An October 1952 article in *Fate,* a popular digest-sized magazine on "true mysteries," drew heavily on the AP piece, citing the Flight 19 story along with others which by the 1960s would evolve into the "Bermuda Triangle" concept. . . .

Unexplained: 347 Strange Sightings, Incredible Occurrences, and Puzzling Phenomena, by Jerome Clark. Copyright © 1993 Visible Ink Press, a Division of Gale Research, Inc. Reprinted by permission of the Gale Group, www.galegroup.com.

GLOSSARY

acknowledge (v.) to admit the existence, reality, or truth of

baffling (adj.) puzzling; frustrating

debris (n.) the scattered remains of something broken or destroyed; wreckage or rubble

deteriorating (adj.) disintegrating

diminished (adj.) smaller and less important

dissension (n.) a difference of opinion, especially one causing strife within a group

frequency (n.) the number of times a certain phenomenon occurs during a particular interval

futile (adj.) useless

hamper (v.) to prevent the free movement, action, or progress of

in vain (adv.) to no avail; without success

kilocycle (n.) a unit that measures frequency

rendezvous (n.) a prearranged meeting

retrieve (v.) to find and carry back; fetch

transmission (n.) the sending of a signal through an electrical device

turbulence (n.) unrest or disturbance

veer (v.) to turn aside from a course, direction, or purpose

QUICK COMPREHENSION CHECK ✓

Review the selection carefully to understand the controlling idea, main points, and most important details. Mark this information or take notes in your course log. Use this information to construct a brief summary paragraph.

_____

_____

_____

_____

_____

_____

_____

_____

_____

_____

_____

_____

_____

_____

_____

_____

_____

QUESTIONS FOR THOUGHT AND DISCUSSION

1. Describe Flight 19—the number and type of aircraft as well as the crew who flew them. Include in your description comments about the crew's experience as pilots.

2. What was Flight 19's mission? What did the aircraft have to accomplish? What was their flight plan?

3. When was the first confusing communication from Flight 19 received? Who sent it? What did it say? Who received it?

4. What problems did this communication reveal? Address three topics in your response: the location of the aircraft, the quality of its communication with other aircraft, and differences of opinion among the Flight 19 crew members.

5. When did people on the ground first become seriously concerned about Flight 19? Why? Be as specific as possible about what was happening on the Flight 19 aircraft and where they were located.

6. Describe the weather conditions as the sun set. Did anyone know where the Flight 19 aircraft were located at this time? Explain.

7. Why was it difficult to dispatch rescue aircraft to assist Flight 19?

   How many rescue units were initially sent to search for Flight 19?

   What happened to them?

8. When was Flight 19 believed to be "down"?

   What physical evidence and debris from the aircraft were discovered?

   What was mysterious about Flight 19?

9. What concept about strange occurrences evolved as a result of Flight 19's disappearance? Given all the information in the selection, is this explanation plausible? What other explanations are possible?

ANOTHER LOOK AT THE SELECTION

"Flight 19" contains a significant amount of detail. To read the selection and comprehend its story line, you had to sort through and organize this detail. This exercise guides you to focus on and examine details about the selection's basic story line: the aircraft's original flight plan and the way it actually flew.

1. Before examining the details about the basic story line, review the number and types of details in the selection. Read the different subtopics in the following list and circle only those that identify the different groups of details that were actually included in the selection.

flight plan	**Flight 19's previous missions**
the crew's families	**where the aircraft were built**
military service	**a chronology of events**
geographic points and distances	**how to fly an Avenger**
the Bermuda Triangle	**rescue craft**
recovering Flight 19 from the ocean	**Flight 19 aircraft**
how to become a pilot	**the crew**

2. Now focus on the categories of details: (a) where Flight 19 was supposed to fly and (b) where it actually flew. Find and mark these details in the selection.

3. Next, use these details to plot the two different paths on the following map. Use two different colors to outline the paths and distinguish them from one another.

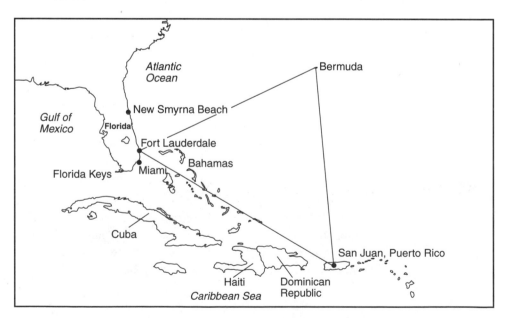

A detailed map of the area over which Flight 19 flew the day it disappeared.

4. Now study the map and answer the following questions:

    a. How far was Flight 19 from its planned course? Circle one:

              not far at all

              very far

              completely off course

    b. Where did Flight 19 deviate from its course? _____

    c. Did Flight 19 really go down in the area known as the Bermuda Triangle?

    _____

    d. Explain whether using details from the selection to mark the map improved your understanding of the selection's main idea.

    _____

    _____

    _____

    _____

    _____

LOOKING BEYOND THE SELECTION

Debunking the Myth

    debunk (v.) to expose false ideas or exaggerated claims

Was the disappearance of Flight 19 really a mysterious event? What other explanations exist? Evaluate the claims about Flight 19 and the Bermuda Triangle, using resources other than the selection. Search through the library and the Internet for additional information. After reviewing a variety of sources, answer the following questions:

    1. What different explanations for the disappearance of Flight 19 exist?

      a. _____

      b. _____

      c. _____

2. What evidence exists for each explanation? What is the quality of this evidence? Enter your information in the table below.

EXPLANATION	EVIDENCE	BELIEVABLE? *YES* OR *NO*

3. Where did you find additional information about Flight 19?

_____

_____

4. What information was most plausible and reliable? Why?

_____

_____

5. How valid were the Web sites you used? Was the information on the Web stated clearly and supported adequately?

_____

_____

_____

6. What is your explanation for the disappearance of Flight 19? Why?

_____

_____

_____

7. Who might disagree with you? How would you defend your viewpoint in a discussion with this person?

_____

_____

_____

_____

_____

_____

VOCABULARY BUILDING

Formulating Position Statements

The reading about Flight 19 and content in other selections have shown you that people have multiple perspectives about a variety of topics. These perspectives vary according to individuals' differing values and experiences. As you continue your study of English, you will practice argument and persuasion in both oral presentations and written work. This practice will help you express your own position on various topics. The following exercise gives you a head start with the vocabulary for this purpose.

1. Look at the following words carefully. Using a dictionary and working with your peers, categorize them as appropriate for **speaking for** or **against** a topic. Then write each word in the proper column in the chart.

embrace	oppose	contest
stand against	welcome	adopt
believe	accept	discredit
disbelieve	support	reject
endorse	disclaim	stand behind
deny	advocate	approve
stand up for	debunk	uphold

STATING OPINIONS

TO SPEAK *FOR* A TOPIC	TO SPEAK *AGAINST* A TOPIC

2. Using four words in the table, write four sentences in which you state your opinion about different selections in this textbook.

a. _____

_____

_____

b. _____

_____

_____

c. _____

_____

_____

d. _____

_____

_____

IN YOUR WORDS

Flight 19: The Official Log

You are an investigator who will spend a great deal of time interviewing people, examining evidence, and reviewing common records to determine what really happened to Flight 19. To get started, you must construct the official log of the flight's communications and location during its mission on the day it disappeared. Start this phase of your investigation now. Use the following chart to construct a chronological record of events reported in the selection.

TIME	EVENT	LOCATION	COMMENTS

SUMMING UP

Share your thoughts about the selection in a group or with the class. What do others think?

1. What did you and your classmates know about the Bermuda Triangle before reading the selection? What do you know about it now? Does everyone accept the mysteries associated with the Bermuda Triangle, or do you believe the concept is a myth? What is the position of the majority of the people in your group or in the class?

2. What explanations did you and your classmates provide to explain the disappearance of Flight 19? What evidence supports the different views? Do you all agree about what happened to Flight 19? If so, summarize this position. If not, identify the major points of disagreement.

3. How is the story of Flight 19 a good foundation for practice with persuasive writing, argument, or debate?

4. What other incidents in the area known as the Bermuda Triangle did you and your classmates learn about when you looked beyond the selection? How did these stories affect you? Did they influence your opinion about the Bermuda Triangle? How? Why?

CLOSING THE CHAPTER

Take a moment to think about the selections you read in this chapter. Evaluate the evidence that appears to support the existence of the strange and the paranormal. What is your position? Why? Are any of the selections more believable than others? Why? Would you like to read more about the chapter's topic? Why?

REFLECTING AND SYNTHESIZING

Class Debates

Use the information and vocabulary from the chapter to organize class debates about the strange and paranormal.

debate (n.) a formal contest of argumentation in which two opposing teams attack and defend a topic

Individual Work

Review your opinions about the chapter's selections, as stated or explored in the preceding exercises. What is your position on the strange and paranormal? Is it one of overriding belief, despite the topic, or does your opinion differ from selection to selection? Think about these questions to prepare for the debate.

Group Work

In class and group discussions, establish the format and procedures for your debate. Determine the following:

- the number of debate groups you will have
- your debate topics—whether you will debate the chapter's broad topic or topics from the selections, from your research and other information you have
- the dates when the debates will take place
- debate groups, if needed
- timekeeping and procedures during the debates
- the roles of different people on a debate team